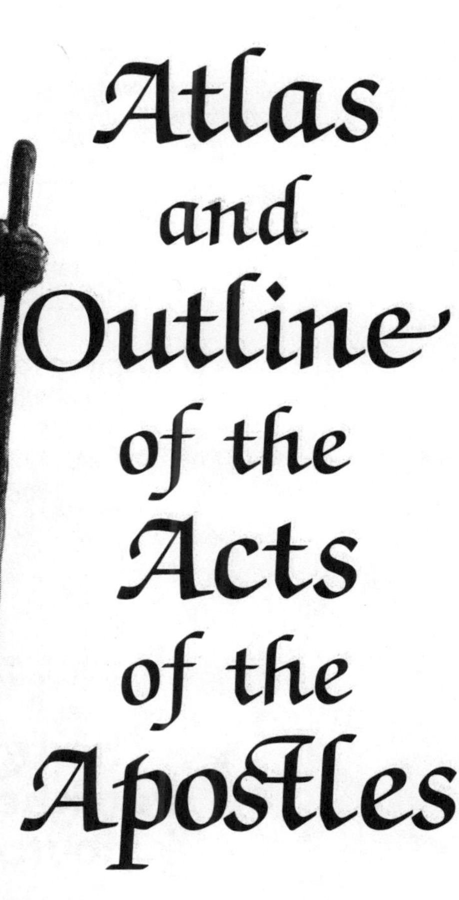

Atlas and Outline of the Acts of the Apostles

Duane S. Crowther

International Standard Book Number
0-88290-219-9

Library of Congress Catalog Card Number
83-80528

Horizon Publishers Catalog and Order Number
1008

Printed and Distributed in the
United States of America
by

Horizon
Publishers &
Distributors, Inc.

50 South 500 West
P.O. Box 490
Bountiful, Utah 84010

PREFACE

The Purpose of This Book—A "Handy Study Guide"

This *Atlas and Outline of the Acts of the Apostles* has been prepared to serve as a simple but detailed guide to studying the history of the New Testament Church. It encompasses the period from Christ's ascension into heaven until the conclusion of the writing of the books of the New Testament—a period of approximately 60 years. The book outlines the book of Acts in detail, then continues past the end of that book to cover the martyrdom of Paul and Peter, the fall of Jerusalem, and the later activities of John and other Church leaders. It is a companion volume to its predecessor: *Atlas and Outline of the Life of Christ.*

From the inception of the project, the challenge has been to keep the book as short and unencumbered as possible, while still recording all the disciples' known travels, sermons, epistles, and other significant experiences detailed or alluded to in the Biblical record and early historical documents. Its preparation has been a labor of love—love for the scriptures, and love for the uplifting influence felt by those who study the words of the Bible and strive to pattern their lives after the precepts and admonitions it contains. It is my desire that it may be a useful and inspirational tool to all who use it.

Like its companion volume, this small book is "loaded" with useful information. Though it is far more comprehensive than any other outline of the activities of the New Testament Church in print at the present time, it is designed to be a "handy study guide," not a profound scholarly work. To maintain its brevity, many interesting historical sidelights have been omitted; yet the book gives brief descriptions of the lives of historical figures, descriptive summaries of numerous locations visited by these individuals, and a host of interesting facts and figures that will make the study of the New Testament more meaningful to the reader. The major objective of the book, however, has been to provide a brief, portable, easily utilized aid to understanding the experiences, travels, and teaching of the early Church leaders.

Problems of Dating and Chronological Order

There are almost as many conflicting views concerning the dating of New Testament events as there are Biblical scholars. A careful study of the dating of various events shows that much of their work consists only of "educated guesses." The dating of each event in this volume certainly must be classified in the same way—I have unearthed no new discoveries which would fix the exact time of the events reported herein.

As this outline was being prepared, I debated whether to include dates, seasons, and chronological relationships. I recognized that many such notes would be expressions of opinion rather than fact; I also realized that this brief outline format would allow little room for documentation or commentary. Yet I felt that the inclusion of these helps would be of value to the reader, and would aid him in making his own observations as he studied the books of the New Testament. While readily acknowledging the possibility of error in the areas of dating and chronology, I still felt that more dating information, rather than less, would be of greatest benefit to the reader. This background is included for every chronological entry. Though it may seem somewhat repetitive to one who reads large portions of the outline, it was included on an every-item basis to accommodate those who will occasionally look up a brief passage without devoting time to an extensive reading of its context.

Uncertainty of Routes Traveled

Another problem exists in the matter of the routes traveled by early Church leaders during their ministry. No one, of course, knows the exact routes they followed in most of their journeys. In some instances the maps included in this book show their travels more or less "as the crow flies," rather than attempting to reproduce the road systems of their day.

Not a Book on Doctrine—Appropriate for All Faiths

This book is not a book on doctrine. It is intended as a historical guide which can benefit Bible students of all religious denominations. Doctrinal questions have been avoided—no effort has been made to take a position on them. Instead, I have been content to identify the existence of doctrinal material in the passages summarized by placing a star (★) at the end of the entry. There is a host of other books which can provide doctrinal commentary on the passages thus identified, and the reader can select those which he feels will best lend understanding to his studies.

Despite the limitations mentioned above, there is much in this brief outline that will be of value to you who use it to study the life and travels of the early Christian leaders. May it prove a blessing in your life, as it has been for me as I prepared it. And may we always be found

In His Service,

Duane S. Crowther

CONTENTS

USE THIS EFFECTIVE MARKING SYSTEM FOR THE ACTS OF THE APOSTLES

Keeping track of the many interrelated events in the New Testament is a challenging task for Bible students. It is even more difficult for casual readers of the holy scriptures. A marking system helps one to locate passages and events quickly and to keep track of related events which are recorded elsewhere in the Bible. Experience has shown that various New Testament books require different marking systems. The challenge in the four gospels, for instance, is to correlate and cross-reference the many events reported in the parallel accounts of the Savior's life. In the *Acts of the Apostles,* there is a single line of events, with many occasional insights added from brief allusions in the epistles. A separate marking system than that used for the four gospels is appropriate—one for the rest of the New Testament, based primarily on the account in Acts.

The outline found in this book can serve as the basis for a simple but very efficient Bible marking system. Since it deals only with chronology, and utilizes only the page margins, it can be easily superimposed over other color codes and doctrinal identification systems. Here's how to set it up in your Bible:

1. **Identify the beginning of each chronological period.** Turn to the beginning of each chapter in this book and find the corresponding passage in your Bible. Then, mark in your Bible, by the first verse of the period, the following information: (1) the period number; (2) the name of the period; (3) the dates of the period; and (4), the beginning and ending references which the period encompasses.

For instance, to record the beginning of Paul's second missionary journey, write the following in the margin of your Bible by Acts 15:36:

Period 7
Paul's Second Missionary Journey
49 A.D.-52 A.D.
Acts 15:36-18:23

2. **Record the period name and / or number at the top of each page.** You may wish to add dates and other information also. Example:

Period 8
Paul's Third Missionary Journey
52 A.D.-57 A.D.

3. **Write the number of each event in the margin beside the verse in which the event begins.** Do this throughout the book of Acts. Example:

139 9 And a vision appeared to
Paul in the night; There
stood a man of Macedonia,
and prayed him, saying,
Come over into Macedonia,
and help us.
10 And after he had seen
the vision, immediately we
endeavoured to go into
Macedonia, assuredly gathering
that the Lord had
called us for to preach the
gospel unto them.

4. **Label each New Testament book with its chronological number.** Since its number relates to the numbering system prepared for the book of Acts, you may wish to write the word Acts with the number. For instance, the writing of 1 Thessalonians was event number 164 in the outline. On the title page for 1 Thessalonians, write:

Acts #164

5. **Label all additions to the book of Acts' list of events found in the various epistles.** To indicate that they are also part of the Acts' numbering system, you may wish to write the word Acts with the number. For instance, Peter's visit to Antioch, recorded in Galatians 2:11-21, is event number 120 in the Acts chronological listing. By Galatians 2:11, write:

Acts 120 11 ¶ But when Peter was
come to Antioch, I withstood
him to the face, because
he was to be blamed.
12 For before that certain
came from James, he did eat

6. **Identify every major discourse by writing the discourse number and complete reference by its beginning verse.** Example:

Discourse #7
Acts 17:16-33

Many people choose to individualize their Bible marking system, and you should feel free to do so also. There is no *right* way to mark a Bible—your system should be one that you feel will best meet your needs. But if you will utilize this system, or some adaptation of it, you will know:

1. Where each new event begins in the Book of Acts.
2. Where every major discourse begins and ends.
3. What period of activity is being discussed.
4. Where every New Testament book fits into the chronological framework.

You'll be completely keyed to this book, which will then serve as a master index to your New Testament. The system can be fully installed in your Bible in less than a day. Do it now, and enjoy it for a lifetime!

Period 1

THE EARLY MINISTRY OF THE APOSTLES IN JERUSALEM

(From the Ascension of Jesus to the Sanhedrin's Prohibition Against Preaching)

30 A.D.

Acts 1:1 to 5:42

The Ascension of Jesus
The Appearance of Two Angels
The Selection of Matthias as the Twelfth Apostle
The Outpouring of the Spirit on the Day of Pentecost
The Conversion of 3,000 New Members
Peter and John Heal a Lame Man in the Temple
5,000 More Converts Believe Peter's Sermon
Peter and John Arrested and Threatened by the Sanhedrin
A Second Outpouring of the Holy Ghost
The Selfishness and Death of Ananias and Sapphira
Signs and Wonders Wrought by the Apostles
The Apostles Arrested, Beaten, and Threatened by the Sanhedrin
The Apostles Released from Prison by an Angel
Gamaliel's Warning to the Sanhedrin

1. Luke's introduction to Theophilus (Acts 1:1).

Note: **The Book of Acts**—Luke, the author of Acts, is the same individual who wrote the third gospel, his "former treatise." He was a physician (Col. 4:14), and was probably a Gentile, who wrote to the Gentiles through Theophilus, his Gentile patron. The book is believed to have been written about 63 A.D., when Luke spent two years with Paul during his imprisonment in Rome.

2. Jesus was seen by his apostles, and instructed them for 40 days after his passion (1:2-3). *Galilee and Jerusalem; April 9 to May 18, 30 A.D.* ★

3. Jesus' final instruction to his apostles (1:4-8). *Mount of Olives, between Jerusalem and Bethany; May 18, 30 A.D.* ★[1]

---

1. This outline is intended as a non-denominational study guide which focuses primarily on historical and geographical aspects of the Acts of the Apostles, rather than on doctrinal issues. However, to aid in the study of doctrinal patterns, stars (★) have been placed by passages containing significant doctrinal items. Major doctrinal discourses have also been identified and numbered.

4. Jesus was taken up, and a cloud received him as his apostles observed his ascension (1:9). *Mount of Olives; the same day, May 18, 30 A.D.* ★

Note: **Traditional Site of Christ's Ascension**—It is generally believed that Christ ascended into heaven from the Mount of Olives, about 3,000 feet east of Jerusalem, near the present site of the Carmelite convent of Pater-Noster. Two churches have been erected on what are believed to be the sites of his ascension: the Russian Tower of the Ascension and the Dome of Ascension. This area is over the crest of the mount, towards Bethany.

5. Two "men" in white apparel appeared to the apostles and told them Jesus will come in like manner as they saw him go into heaven (1:10-11). *Mount of Olives; the same day, May 18, 30 A.D.* ★

6. The apostles returned from the Mount of Olives to Jerusalem. They went into an upper room which was the abode of the eleven remaining apostles (1:12-13). *Jerusalem; the same day, May 18, 30 A.D.*

Note: **The Upper Room**—The location of the upper room in Jerusalem is unknown. If it was like typical buildings of the time, it was a roof chamber furnished as a retreat. It was probably approached by climbing stone steps attached to the outside wall of the house.

7. The apostles continued in prayer and supplication, united with the woman, Mary (the mother of Jesus) and with his brethren (1:14). *Jerusalem; mid May, 30 A.D.* ★

8. Peter's discourse to 120 disciples concerning the choosing of another apostle: "One must be ordained to be a witness with us of his resurrection" **(1:15-22).** *Jerusalem; late May, 30 A.D.* ★

9. The selection of Matthias to be the twelfth apostle (1:23-26). *Jerusalem; late May, 30 A.D.* ★

10. The Holy Ghost was poured out upon all the assembled disciples on the Day of Pentecost. They were filled and began to speak with other tongues (2:1-4). *Jerusalem; morning of May 28, 30 A.D. (fifty days after Christ's resurrection, if it was on the Passover, and 10 days following his ascension into heaven).* ★

Note: **The Day of Pentecost**—Pentecost is the Hellenistic name for the Hebrew Feast of Weeks, described in Leviticus 23:15-21. It was held at the time of the corn harvest, and occurred 50 days after the first day of Passover (Easter). This day opened a new era for the Church, and the real beginning of its work of proclaiming the gospel to all mankind. The outpouring of the Spirit brought unity and power to the Church and brought immediate growth to the community of believers.

11. A multitude of devout Jews from many nations assembled when word of the outpouring of the Holy Spirit was noised abroad. They marvelled how the disciples from Galilee could suddenly speak in so many languages (2:5-13). *Jerusalem; morning of the Day of Pentecost, May 28, 30 A.D.* ★

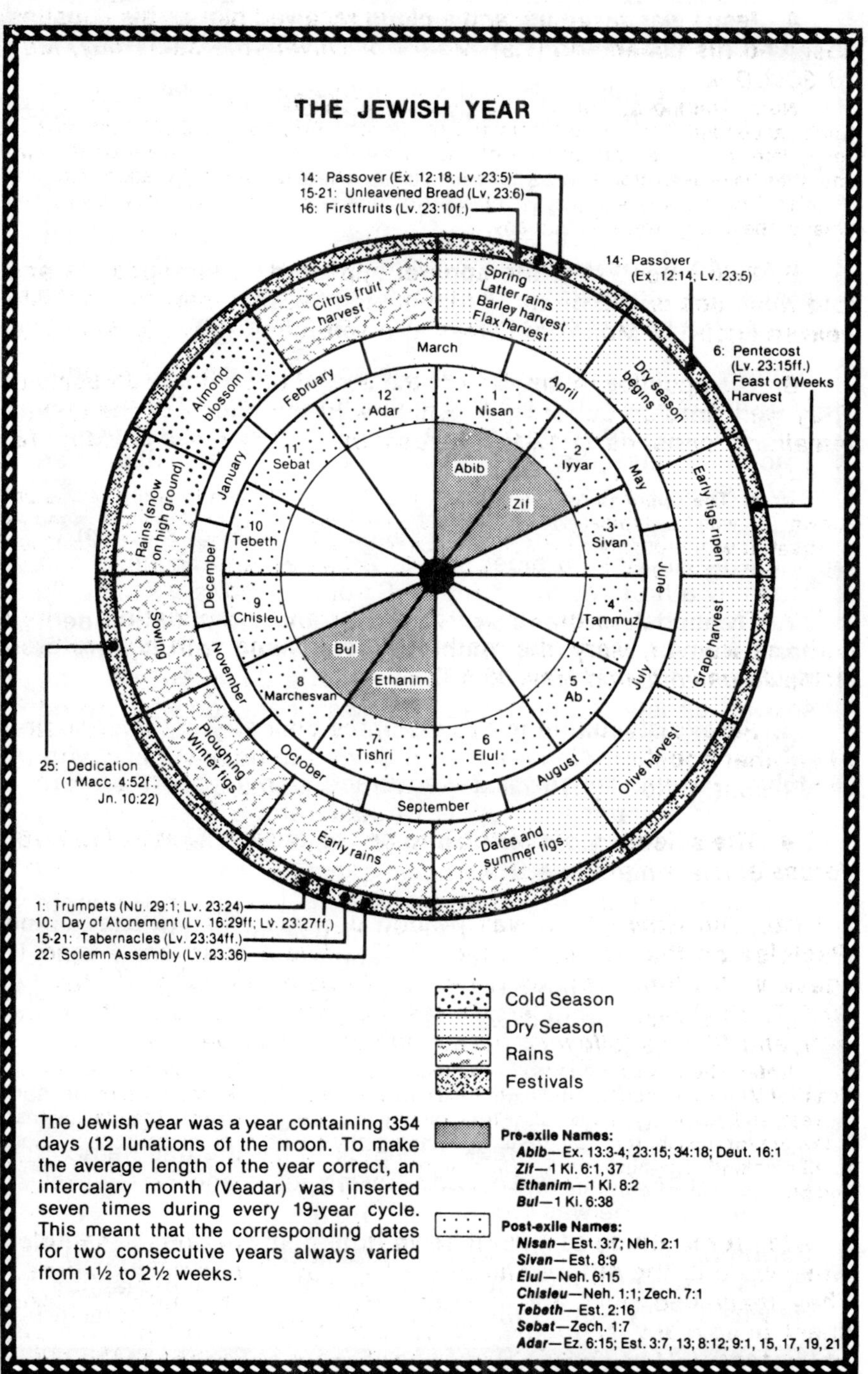
THE JEWISH YEAR
14: Passover (Ex. 12:18; Lv. 23:5)
15-21: Unleavened Bread (Lv. 23:6)
16: Firstfruits (Lv. 23:10f.)
14: Passover (Ex. 12:14; Lv. 23:5)
6: Pentecost (Lv. 23:15ff.) Feast of Weeks Harvest
25: Dedication (1 Macc. 4:52f.; Jn. 10:22)
1: Trumpets (Nu. 29:1; Lv. 23:24)
10: Day of Atonement (Lv. 16:29ff; Lv. 23:27ff.)
15-21: Tabernacles (Lv. 23:34ff.)
22: Solemn Assembly (Lv. 23:36)
Spring Latter rains Barley harvest Flax harvest
Dry season begins
Early figs ripen
Grape harvest
Olive harvest
Dates and summer figs
Early rains
Ploughing Winter figs
Sowing
Rains (snow on high ground)
Almond blossom
Citrus fruit harvest
March
April
May
June
July
August
September
October
November
December
January
February
1 Nisan
2 Iyyar
3 Sivan
4 Tammuz
5 Ab
6 Elul
7 Tishri
8 Marchesvan
9 Chisleu
10 Tebeth
11 Sebat
12 Adar
Abib
Zif
Bul
Ethanim
Cold Season
Dry Season
Rains
Festivals
The Jewish year was a year containing 354 days (12 lunations of the moon. To make the average length of the year correct, an intercalary month (Veadar) was inserted seven times during every 19-year cycle. This meant that the corresponding dates for two consecutive years always varied from 1½ to 2½ weeks.
Pre-exile Names:
Abib—Ex. 13:3-4; 23:15; 34:18; Deut. 16:1
Zif—1 Ki. 6:1, 37
Ethanim—1 Ki. 8:2
Bul—1 Ki. 6:38
Post-exile Names:
Nisan—Est. 3:7; Neh. 2:1
Sivan—Est. 8:9
Elul—Neh. 6:15
Chisleu—Neh. 1:1; Zech. 7:1
Tebeth—Est. 2:16
Sebat—Zech. 1:7
Adar—Ez. 6:15; Est. 3:7, 13; 8:12; 9:1, 15, 17, 19, 21

THE TWELVE APOSTLES OF JESUS CHRIST

Simon Peter *(rock)*—Simon was the son of Jonah and the brother of Andrew. He was born in Bethsaida, but lived during Christ's ministry in a house in Capernaum with his wife and mother-in-law. He was a well-to-do fisherman in partnership with his father Jonah, Zebedee, Andrew, James and John. With James and John, he was in the inner circle of disciples closest to Jesus. He was the leader of the Church after Jesus' ascension, and wrote the two epistles of Peter. Tradition states that he was crucified upside down in Rome.

Andrew *(Manly)*—Andrew was the son of Jonah and Joanna, and Simon's brother. He was a disciple of John the Baptist, and was probably the first to be called as Jesus' apostle. Tradition states that he was crucified in Achaia, tied to an X-shaped cross.

James *(James the Great.* His name is the English form of Jacob.)—He was an older son of Zebedee and Salome, and probably a first cousin of Jesus (Salome was Mary's sister?). Jesus called James and John "Boanerges" (sons of thunder). James was the second disciple of the inner circle, and is believed to be the father of the apostle Jude. He was the second apostle to be killed, and was beheaded by Herod Agrippa (Acts 12:2).

John—He was the son of Zebedee and Salome, and therefore a brother of James, an uncle of Jude, and a first cousin of Jesus. He was called "the beloved," and was the third member of the inner circle. He was a fisherman, and a disciple of John the Baptist. He owned a home in Jerusalem. He wrote the gospel of John, the three epistles of John, and the book of Revelation. Jesus gave him the responsibility from the cross of caring for his mother. John preached in Ephesus, was exiled to Patmos, and was last heard of in Ephesus about 100 A.D. (See Mt. 27:3-5.)

Philip *(lover of horses)*—Philip was from Bethsaida and was a close friend of John and Andrew. He was a liberal Jew, and must have had some Greek influence in his life (his name is Greek and he served as a liason between Jesus and the Greeks). Tradition says he was crucified in Phrygia.

Bartholomew—Also known as **Nathanael** *(God has given)*—He was a son of Tolmai, from Cana, and of the tribe of Naphtali. He was usually named with Philip, and was called "an Israelite without guile" by Jesus. According to tradition, he was flayed, beheaded, or crucified in India or Armenia.

Thomas—Also called **Didymus** *(twin)*—He was a fisherman from Bethsaida, and a boyhood friend of John. Tradition states that he was killed by a lance in India or Persia.

Matthew—Also known as **Levi** *(gift of God)*—He was the son of Alphaeus and a brother of James the lesser, from Capernaum, and probably of the tribe of Levi. He was educated a Publican and tax collector in Capernaum, and was wealthy. He wrote the gospel of Matthew. Tradition asserts that he was killed by fire, sword or spear in Ethiopia.

James—A brother of Matthew, he was the son of Alphaeus and Mary (she is also identified as the wife of Cleophaus, another form of Alphaeus). He was from Capernaum, and of the tribe of Levi. His mother was probably a first cousin of Mary, the mother of Jesus. He may have been a Zealot. He was known as James the lesser, probably because he was younger or smaller than James the son of Zebedee. He is not James the brother of Jesus, who wrote the epistle of James and was leader of the Church in Jerusalem. Tradition confuses his death with that of Jesus' brother—one or both of them were thrown off the temple wall and then beaten to death by the Jews.

Lebbaeus *(hearty)*—Also known as **Thaddaeus** *(dear one)* and **Jude** (a derivitive of "Judah").—He was called the brother of James (Lk. 6:16). Tradition says he was the son of James the greater, thus being the grandson of Zebedee and the nephew of John, and first cousin once removed of Jesus. He was a fisherman, and of the tribe of Judah. He should not be confused with the brother of Jesus (Mt. 13:55). Tradition says he was crucified at Edessa or Persia.

Simon—Also called **Zelotes**—He was a fisherman from Cana, and probably was a member of the Zealots, a nationalistic sect that sought the overthrow of both the Jewish and Roman jurisdictions (this was the direct opposite of Matthew's views as a Publican). According to tradition, he preached in Britain and was crucified either in Britain or Persia.

Matthias—This disciple was chosen by lot to take the place of Judas Iscariot (Acts 1:23-26). His name, a shortened form of Mattathias, meant "gift of Yahweh." There is no reliable historical information concerning him.

12. Peter's discourse to the Jewish multitude: "Jesus hath God raised up, whereof we are all witnesses . . . God hath made that same Jesus, whom ye have crucified, both Lord and Christ" **(2:14-36).** *Jerusalem; morning of the Day of Pentecost, May 28, 30 A.D.* ***[★ — Major Discourse #1]***

Note: **The Third Hour**—In the Jewish time system, a daylight hour was always one-twelfth of the period of daylight, and the numbering began with sunrise. The third hour, then, was still quite early in the morning, about 9:00. On festival days the Jews would eat nothing until their morning synagogue service was completed.

THE JEWISH AND ROMAN TIME SYSTEM

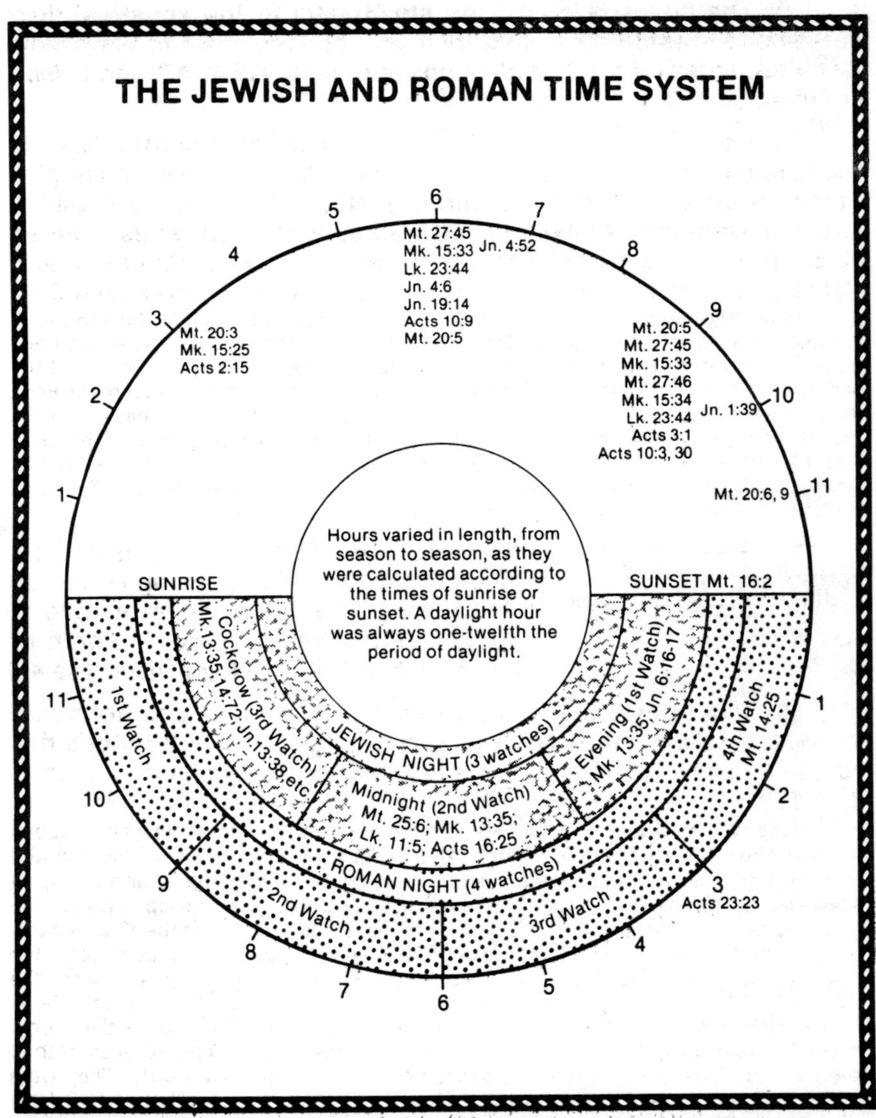

13. Peter's response to the multitude's question, "What shall we do?": "Repent and be baptized every one of you in the name of Jesus Christ for the remission of sins, and ye shall receive the gift of the Holy Ghost" **(2:37-40).** *Jerusalem; morning of the Day of Pentecost, May 28, 30 A.D.* ★

14. The multitude that received his word were baptized; that same day about 3,000 souls were added to the Church (2:41). *Jerusalem; the Day of Pentecost, May 28, 30 A.D.* ★

15. The converts continued steadfastly in the apostles' doctrine and fellowship. They sold their possessions, gave to the needy, then lived together and had all things in common (2:42-47). *Jerusalem; summer, 30 A.D.* ★

16. Peter and John healed a lame man at the Beautiful Gate of the temple: "Silver and gold have I none; but such as I have give I thee: In the name of Jesus Christ of Nazareth rise up and walk." **The man went into the temple and praised God. A crowd assembled at Solomon's porch (3:1-11).** *Jerusalem, the Gate Beautiful and Solomon's Porch; the ninth hour (mid-afternoon), summer, 30 A.D.* ★

***Note:* The Temple of Herod**—Herod the Great began to rebuild the Temple of Zerubabbel in 19 B.C., during the 18th year of his reign. The temple proper was completed in 18 months by a work force of 1,000 specially trained priests. The rest of the temple took many years to finish, and the final touches were still not complete when the temple was destroyed by the Romans in 70 A.D. The temple was made of white marble and gold, with beautifully ornamented porches and courtyards. The Gate Beautiful opened into one of the outer courts on the eastern side of the temple. Solomon's Porch was the name given to the eastern cloisters of the temple. The early Christians made it their gathering place and assembled there daily.

17. Peter's discourse in the temple: "Repent . . . and be converted, that your sins may be blotted out . . . God, having raised up his Son Jesus, sent him to bless you, in turning away every one of you from his iniquities" **(3:12-26).** *Jerusalem, Solomon's Porch of the Temple; mid-afternoon, summer, 30 A.D.* ***[★ —Major Discourse #2]***

18. The priests and Sadducees arrested Peter and John and imprisoned them overnight, but about 5,000 who heard Peter's discourse believed (4:1-4). *Jerusalem; evening of the same day, summer, 30 A.D.* ★

***Note:* Sadducees and Pharisees**—These were the two main Jewish religious sects in the time of the early church. The *Sadducees* accepted only the law and rejected oral tradition; they denied resurrection, immortality, angels, and the spirit world (Mk. 12:18; Lk. 20:27; Acts 23:8). They were a relatively small group, but were the elite, and held and controlled the office of high priest. They supported the Maccabeans, but looked mostly to Rome for support. They were denounced by both John the Baptist and Jesus. The *Pharisees* were the most influential party, and were the strictest of the Jewish sects (the "separatists," who supposedly separated themselves from evil). They wore distinguishing clothing so they could be easily recognized. They believed in Jewish tradition, as well as law, and pledged to obey both in every detail. They were constantly concerned about ceremonial purity. They were hostile to foreign rule. They looked for a Messiah to come, but saw that coming from a very nationalistic viewpoint. They believed in predestination, immortality, the spirit world, revelation, that the spirits of the wicked were imprisoned forever under the earth, and that the virtuous would rise again and even migrate to other bodies. They believed they were the only interpreters of God's word. Jesus condemned their long public prayers, frequent fasts, arrogance, hypocrisy, impenitence, and their emphasis on salvation by works. They were closely allied with the scribes and lawyers.

19. Annas, Caiaphas, John and Alexander, representing the office of high priest, questioned Peter and John (4:5-7). *Jerusalem; the next day, summer, 30 A.D.*

***Note:* The Office of High Priest**—Annas (abbreviated form of Hananiah) was appointed high priest (the highest Jewish religious office) in 7 A.D. by the Roman legate Quirinius, but was deposed in 15 A.D. by Valerius Gratus. As was the Jewish custom, he kept his title "high priest" after being removed from office. Five of his sons also became Jewish high priests. Joseph Caiaphas, son-in-law of Annas, actually served as high priest from 18-36 A.D., though Annas continued to exercise power and influence through him.

20. Peter's response to the high priest's question "By what power, or by what name, have ye done this?": "By the name of Jesus Christ . . . doth this man stand here before you whole" **(4:7-12).** *Jerusalem; the same day, summer, 30 A.D.* ★

21. The high priest and council threatened the apostles, "and commanded them not to speak at all nor teach in the name of Jesus" (4:13-18). *Jerusalem; the same day, summer, 30 A.D.*

22. Peter's and John's reply: "Whether it be right in the sight of God to hearken unto you more than unto God, judge ye. For we cannot but speak the things which we have seen and heard" **(4:19-20).** *Jerusalem; the same day, summer, 30 A.D.* ★

23. Peter and John were released. They went to their own company and reported all that the chief priests and elders had said (4:21-23). *Jerusalem; the same day, summer, 30 A.D.*

24. The prayer of the disciples: "Grant unto thy servants, that with all boldness they may speak thy word . . . and that signs and wonders may be done by the name of thy holy child Jesus" **(4:24-30).** *Jerusalem; the same day, summer, 30 A.D.* ★

25. When they had prayed, the place was shaken, and they were all filled with the Holy Ghost and spoke the word of God with boldness (4:31). *Jerusalem; the same day, summer, 30 A.D.* ★

26. The believers were united and had all things in common. They sold their possessions and gave their income to the apostles for distribution to those that were needy (4:32-35). *Jerusalem; summer, 30 A.D.* ★

27. Joses (Barnabas, a Levite from Cyprus) sold his land, and gave the money to the apostles (4:36-37). *Jerusalem; summer, 30 A.D.*

***Note:* Barnabas**—When Joseph of Cyprus, a Levite, sold his estate and gave the money to the struggling Christian community, the disciples apparently gave him the surname Barnabas, meaning "son of comfort." The island of Cyprus had been the home of many Jews, for several centuries dating back to the time of Alexander the Great. Some scholars believe that Barnabas was educated in Tarsus, and may have known Saul there. The two later became missionary companions as they carried the gospel to Galatia.

28. Ananias and his wife Sapphira sold a possession, but held back part of the price from the apostles. Peter challenged them: "Why hast Satan filled thine heart to lie to the Holy Ghost, and to keep back part of the price of the land?" **Both of them fell down and died, and great fear came upon all the church (5:1-11).** *Jerusalem; summer, 30 A.D.* ★

29. Many signs and wonders were wrought by the apostles. The multitudes brought their sick to Peter in Solomon's Porch of the temple, and the sick were healed. Multitudes of men and women believers were added to the Lord (5:12-16). *Jerusalem, Temple of Herod; summer, 30 A.D.* ★

30. The high priest and the Sadducees had the apostles seized and placed in the common prison. An angel opened the prison doors by night and commanded the apostles: "Go, stand and speak in the temple all the words of this life." **They went to the temple early the next morning and taught (5:17-21).** *Jerusalem, Temple of Herod; summer, 30 A.D.* ★

31. The high priest called the Sanhedrin into session and called for the prisoners. It was discovered that they were not in the prison but were preaching in the temple. The apostles were brought before the council without violence (5:21-27). *Jerusalem, meeting hall of the Sanhedrin; early morning, summer, 30 A.D.*

Note: **The Sanhedrin**—The Jewish senate was also the highest court in both ecclesiastical and civil disputes. It consisted of 71 members, including the high priest who presided over it, and drew its members from the Jewish aristocracy: the chief priests, the scribes, and the elders. Most of its members were either Pharisees or Sadducees, and the Pharisees were in the majority. The Sanhedrin had great power and its own police officers. Its decisions were regarded as binding throughout the Jewish world, though the Roman authority still superseded it.

32. Peter's defense before the Sanhedrin: "We ought to obey God rather than men . . . God . . . raised up Jesus, . . . and we are his witnesses of these things" **(5:27-33).***Jerusalem, meeting hall of the Sanhedrin; the same day, early morning, summer, 30 A.D.* ★

33. Gamaliel, a member of the Sanhedrin, cautioned the council: "If this counsel or this work be of man, it will come to nought: but if it be of God, ye cannot overthrow it; lest haply ye be found even to fight against God." **(5:34-39).** *Jerusalem, meeting hall of the Sanhedrin; the same day, early morning, summer, 30 A.D.*

Note: **Gamaliel**—This learned man was a Pharisee, a doctor of the law, and a distinguished and highly respected teacher. He was the most influential rabbi of his day. He was a grandson (or son) of the great rabbi Hillel. Paul studied from him during his youth (Acts 22:3), and said that he was "taught according to the perfect manner of the law of the fathers, and was zealous toward God" because of his influence.

34. The Sanhedrin commanded the apostles not to speak in the name of Jesus, then beat them and released them. The apostles taught and preached Jesus Christ in the temple and houses daily (5:40-42). *Jerusalem; summer, 30 A.D.* ★

THE JEWISH HIGH PRIESTS
From Herod the Great to the Fall of Jerusalem and the End of the Second Jewish Commonwealth

High Priest	*Appointed By*
Ananel, 37-36 B.C., 34 B.C.?	Herod the Great
Aristobulus III, 35 B.C.	
Jesus, son of Phiabi, ?-22 B.C.	
Simon, son of Boethus, 22-5 B.C.	
Matthias, son of Theophilus, 5-4 B.C.	
Joseph, son of Elam, 5 B.C.	
Joezer, son of Boethus, 4 B.C.	
Eleazar, son of Boethus, 4 B.C.-?	Herod Archelaus
Jesus, son of Sie, ?-A.D. 6	
Annas, A.D. 6-15	Quirinius
Ishmael, son of Phiabi I, A.D. 15-16	Valerius Gratus
Eleazar, son of Annas, A.D. 16-17	
Simon, son of Kamithos, A.D. 17-18	
Joseph Caiaphas, A.D. 18-37	
Jonathan, son of Annas, A.D. 37	Vitellius
Theophilus, son of Annas, A.D. 37-41	
Simon Kantheras, son of Boethus, A.D. 41-?	Herod Agrippa I
Matthias, son of Annas, ?	
Elionaius, son of Kantheras, ?	
Joseph, son of Kami, ?	Herod Agrippa II
Ananias, son of Nebedaius, A.D. 47-55?	
Ishmael, son of Phiabi III, A.D. 55-61?	
Joseph Qabi, son of Simon, A.D. 61-62	
Ananus, son of Ananus, A.D. 62	
Jesus, son of Damnaius, A.D. 62-65	
Joshua, son of Gamaliel, A.D. 63-65	
Matthias, son of Theophilus, A.D. 65-67	
Phinnias, son of Samuel, A.D. 67-70	the people

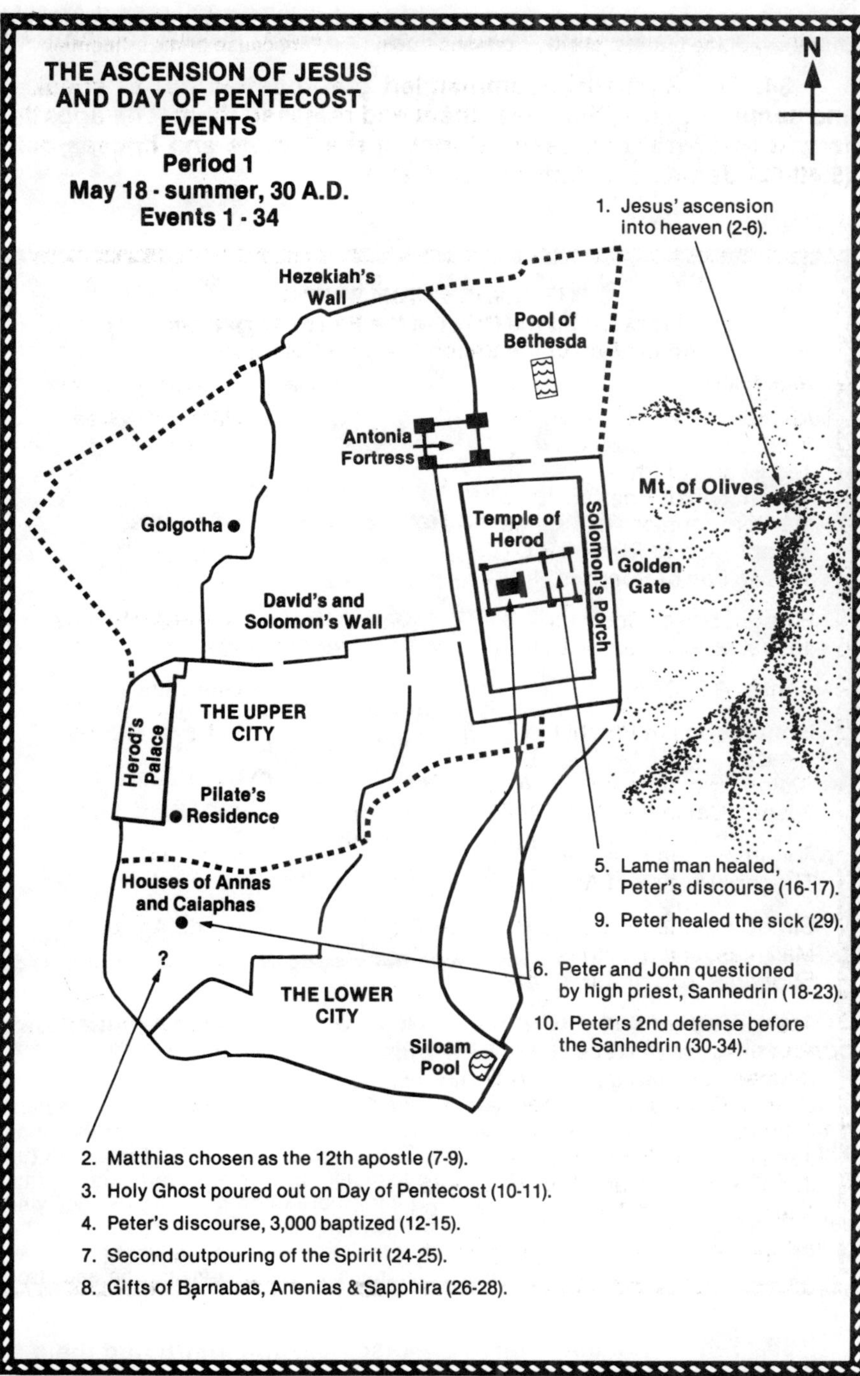

THE ASCENSION OF JESUS
AND DAY OF PENTECOST
EVENTS
Period 1
May 18 - summer, 30 A.D.
Events 1 - 34
N
1. Jesus' ascension into heaven (2-6).
Hezekiah's Wall
Pool of Bethesda
Antonia Fortress
Mt. of Olives
Golgotha
Temple of Herod
Solomon's Porch
Golden Gate
David's and Solomon's Wall
THE UPPER CITY
Herod's Palace
Pilate's Residence
Houses of Annas and Caiaphas
?
THE LOWER CITY
Siloam Pool
5. Lame man healed, Peter's discourse (16-17).
9. Peter healed the sick (29).
6. Peter and John questioned by high priest, Sanhedrin (18-23).
10. Peter's 2nd defense before the Sanhedrin (30-34).
2. Matthias chosen as the 12th apostle (7-9).
3. Holy Ghost poured out on Day of Pentecost (10-11).
4. Peter's discourse, 3,000 baptized (12-15).
7. Second outpouring of the Spirit (24-25).
8. Gifts of Barnabas, Anenias & Sapphira (26-28).

Period 2

EARLY MISSIONARY ACTIVITIES OF THE DISCIPLES

(From the Greek-Hebrew Dispute to the End of Philip's Mission at Caesarea)

30 A.D. to 33 A.D.

Acts 6:1 to 8:40

Dispute of the Greek and Hebrew Members
The Choosing of the Seven Priesthood Bearers
Stephen's Defense Before the Sanhedrin
Stephen's Vision of The Father and The Son
The Stoning of Stephen
Saul Consents to Stephen's Death
Saul Commits Church Members to Prison
Persecution and Scattering of the Church
Philip's Mission to Samaria
Peter and John Rebuke Simon the Magician in Samaria
An Angel Sends Philip South to the Gaza Road
Philip Converts and Baptizes the Ethiopian Eunuch
Philip Is Caught Away by the Spirit to Azotus
Philip's Preaching Throughout the Coastal Cities

35. There arose a dispute between Greek and Hebrew members concerning neglect of the Greek widows (6:1). *Jerusalem; 30-31 A.D.*

Note: **Differences Between Greeks and Hebrews**—The Greek members of the church, or "Hellenists," were educated in the Greek manner, which taught them to question, rethink old concepts, and use logic. Many were raised outside of Palestine, and had foreign parents and backgrounds. They used the Greek Old Testament (the Septuagint), knew Greek literature and philosophy, and were more liberal in their attitude toward the gentile world than were the Hebrews. In many cases they were better educated than were their Hebrew brothers in the gospel. The "Hebrews," or regular Jewish members, were more strict in their approach to the church and their manner of living, retaining much of the rigidness of the Pharisees, the sect from which most of them were converts.

36. The twelve assembled the disciples and instructed them to select seven men for the apostles to appoint to handle the daily

ministration of food. The disciples choose Stephen, Philip, Prochorus, Nicanor, Timon, Parmenas, and Nicolas. The apostles prayed and laid their hands on them (6:1-6). *Jerusalem; 30-31 A.D.* ★

37. The word of God increased and the number of disciples in Jerusalem multiplied greatly. Many of the priests were obedient to the faith (6:7). *Jerusalem; 30-33 A.D.*

38. Stephen did great wonders and miracles. When members of the synagogue of the Libertines were unable to resist his wisdom and spirit, they stirred up the people and elders and scribes, and brought Stephen before the Sanhedrin, where he was accused of blasphemy by false witnesses (6:8-15). *Jerusalem; 33 A.D.* ★

Note: **Libertines, Cyrenians, and Alexandrians**—Libertines were "freedmen"—descendants of Jews who had been carried to Rome by Pompey and other Roman leaders, and then had been freed from their slavery and allowed to return to their homeland. Cyrenians were descendants of the Jewish colony in Cyrene, the capital of Upper Libya. Alexandrians were descendants of the Jewish colony at Alexandria, Egypt. It was there that the Old Testament had been translated into Greek. In that area there was an extensive intermixing of Greek philosophy with Jewish beliefs.

39. Stephen's defense before the Sanhedrin: "Ye do always resist the Holy Ghost. . . . ye have been now the betrayers and murderers . . . of the Just One [Jesus Christ]" **(7:1-54).** *Jerusalem, meeting hall of the Sanhedrin; 33 A.D.* ***[★ —Major Discourse #3]***

40. Stephen, filled with the Holy Ghost, looked up steadfastly into heaven, and saw the glory of God, and Jesus standing on the right hand of God (7:55-56). *Jerusalem, meeting hall of the Sanhedrin; the same day, 33 A.D.* ★

41. The Sanhedrin cast Stephen out of the city and stoned him. Stephen's last words: "Lord Jesus, receive my spirit. . . . Lord, lay not this sin to their charge" **(7:57-60).** *Outside Jerusalem; the same day, 33 A.D.* ★

Note: **Stoning**—The usual procedure was to give the condemned individual a strong drink of wine. Then the witnesses would bind his hands and feet and lead him to the place of stoning. There the witnesses would take a large stone, heavy enough to cause death, and together lay it on the condemned man's heart, acting in unison lest one should act before another (see Deut. 17:6-7), and then the rest of the people would cast stones at the condemned person.

Note: **The Stoning of Stephen**—Stephen's stoning apparently did not follow this procedure. It was illegal, for the Sanhedrin pronounced no formal sentence, and the Roman authorities did not give permission for him to be put to death by the Jews (see John 18:31). Two different Christian traditions identify different Jerusalem gates as the areas where he was stoned. One tradition identifies St. Stephen's gate as the Lion's Gate, or Saint Mary's Gate, on the east wall opposite the Mount of Olives, just north of the Golden Gate. The other tradition places the site on the northwest side of the city, near what is now known as the Damascus Gate.

42. The witnesses to Stephen's death laid down their clothes at the feet of a young man whose name was Saul. Saul was consenting unto his death (7:58; 8:1). *Outside Jerusalem; the same day, 33 A.D.*

43. Devout men buried Stephen, and made great lamentation over him (8:2). *Outside Jerusalem; the same day, 33 A.D.*

44. There was a great persecution against the church at Jerusalem after the stoning of Stephen. The members were all scattered throughout Judea and Samaria except for the apostles (8:1). *Jerusalem, Judea and Samaria; 33-46 A.D.*

45. Saul made havoc of the church, entering into every house and committing the men and women members to prison (8:3). *Jerusalem, Judea and Samaria; 33 A.D.*

46. The scattered members went everywhere preaching the word (8:4). *33-46 A.D.*

47. Philip preached Christ to the people of Samaria. The people gave heed to him because they saw him cast out unclean spirits and heal the lame (8:5-8). *Samaria; 33 A.D.* ★

48. Simon the sorcerer, whom the people previously believed held the power of God, was converted by Philip in Samaria (8:9-13). *Samaria; 33 A.D.* ★

49. The apostles sent Peter and John to Samaria when they heard of Philip's conversions. The apostles laid their hands on the converts and they received the Holy Ghost (8:14-17). *Jerusalem to Samaria; 33 A.D.* ★

50. Simon attempted to buy priesthood power from the apostles, but Peter rebuked him, saying, "Thy money perish with thee, because thou hast thought that the gift of God may be purchased with money. . . . thy heart is not right in the sight of God" **(8:11-24).** *Samaria, 33 A.D.* ★

51. Peter and John preached the gospel in many Samaritan villages and returned to Jerusalem (8:25). *Throughout Samaria and back to Jerusalem; 33 A.D.*

52. An angel appeared to Philip and told him to go south to the desert road from Jerusalem to Gaza. Philip went, and was led by the Spirit to an Ethopian government official (a eunuch who was responsible for Ethiopian queen Candace's treasure), who was returning to Ethiopia from a visit to Jerusalem (8:26-29). *Samaria to Jerusalem to the Gaza road; 33 A.D.* ★

53. Philip heard the official read Isaiah (Isa. 53:7-8) and "preached unto him Jesus." When they passed water, the official asked if he could be baptized. They both went down into the water and Philip baptized him (8:30-38). *The Gaza road; 33 A.D.* ★

54. The Spirit of the Lord caught away Philip. He was found at Azotus, and preached in all the cities till he came to Caesarea (8:39-40). *Coastal road to Caesarea; 33 A.D.* ★

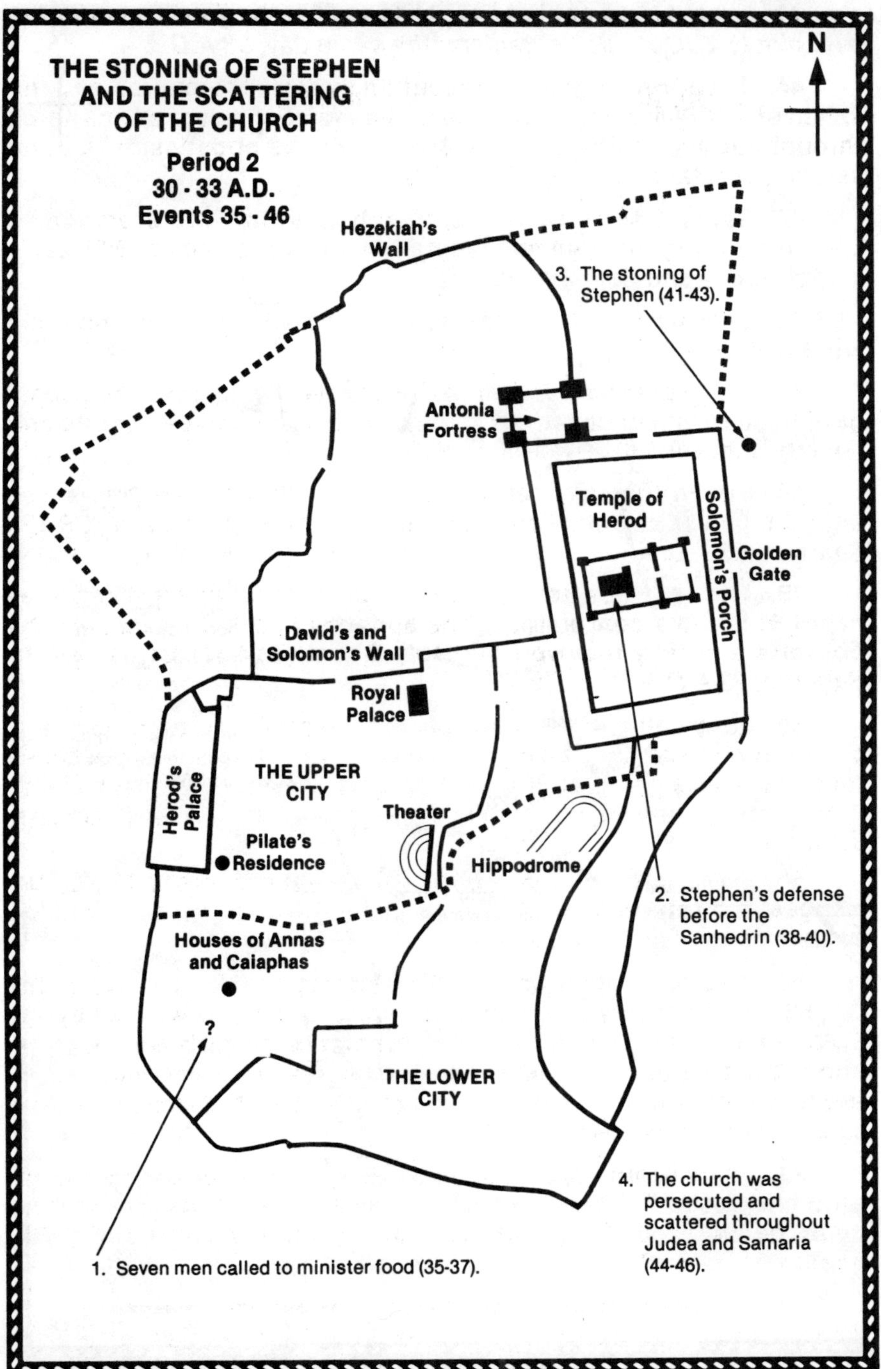
THE STONING OF STEPHEN
AND THE SCATTERING
OF THE CHURCH
Period 2
30 - 33 A.D.
Events 35 - 46
N
Hezekiah's
Wall
3. The stoning of
Stephen (41-43).
Antonia
Fortress
Temple of
Herod
Solomon's Porch
Golden
Gate
David's and
Solomon's Wall
Royal
Palace
Herod's
Palace
THE UPPER
CITY
Theater
Pilate's
Residence
Hippodrome
2. Stephen's defense
before the
Sanhedrin (38-40).
Houses of Annas
and Caiaphas
?
THE LOWER
CITY
4. The church was
persecuted and
scattered throughout
Judea and Samaria
(44-46).
1. Seven men called to minister food (35-37).

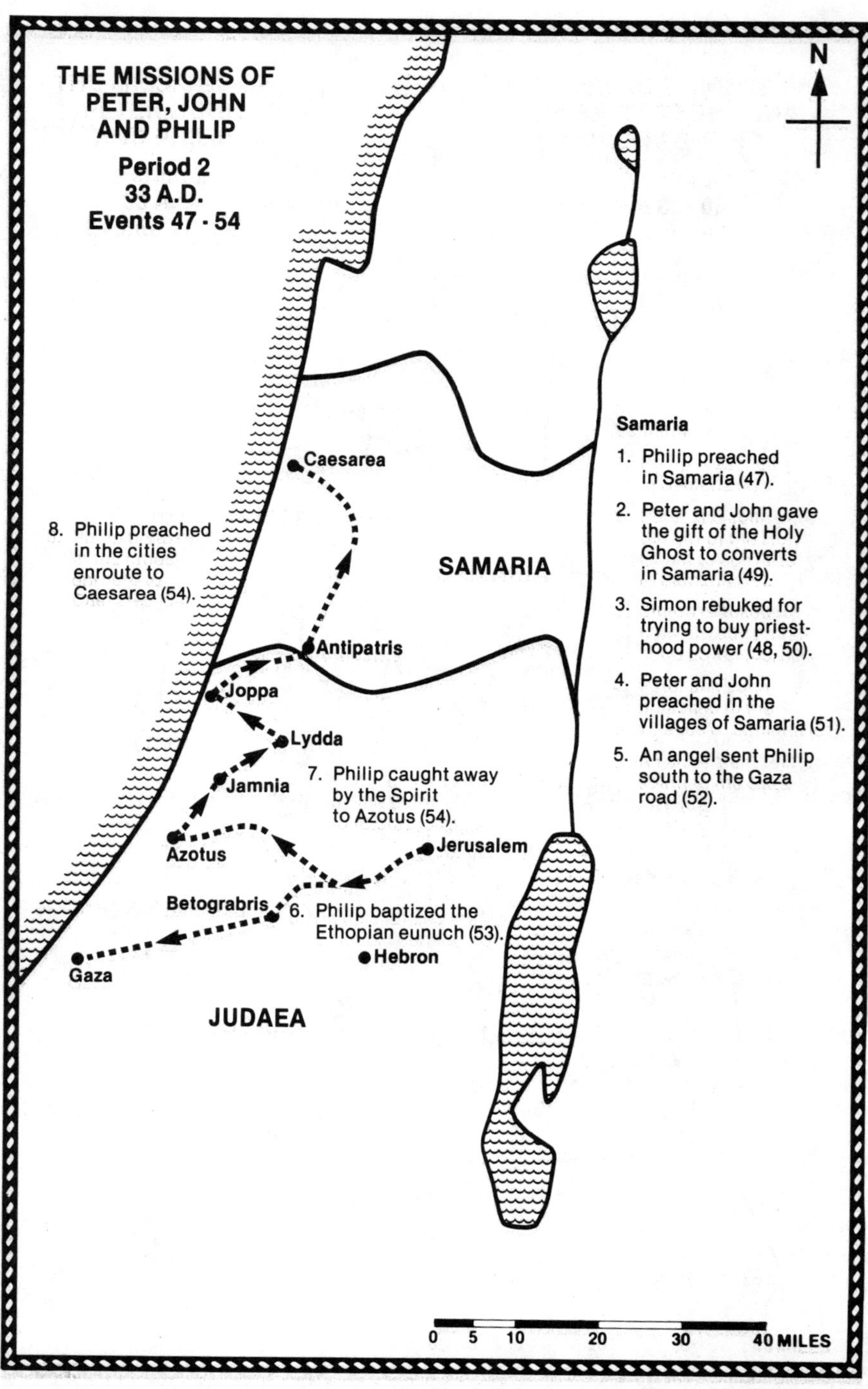
THE MISSIONS OF
PETER, JOHN
AND PHILIP
Period 2
33 A.D.
Events 47 - 54
N
Samaria
1. Philip preached in Samaria (47).
2. Peter and John gave the gift of the Holy Ghost to converts in Samaria (49).
3. Simon rebuked for trying to buy priest-hood power (48, 50).
4. Peter and John preached in the villages of Samaria (51).
5. An angel sent Philip south to the Gaza road (52).
Caesarea
8. Philip preached in the cities enroute to Caesarea (54).
SAMARIA
Antipatris
Joppa
Lydda
Jamnia
7. Philip caught away by the Spirit to Azotus (54).
Azotus
Jerusalem
Betograbris
6. Philip baptized the Ethopian eunuch (53).
Hebron
Gaza
JUDAEA
0 5 10 20 30 40 MILES

Period 3

SAUL'S CONVERSION AND EARLY MINISTRY

(From His Conversion on the Damascus Road to His Flight to Tarsus)

34 A.D. to 42 A.D.

Acts 9:1 to 9:31

Saul's Confrontation with Christ on the Road to Damascus
Ananias Is Sent to Restore Saul's Sight and Baptize Him
Saul's Visit to Arabia
Saul's Escape from the Jews at Damascus
Saul Is Introduced to the Apostles at Jerusalem
Saul's Vision of Jesus in the Temple
Saul Is Sent to Tarsus to Escape the Grecians
Saul's "Hidden Years" in Tarsus
Saul's Visions of the Third Heaven and of Paradise

55. Saul met with the high priest and obtained letters to the synagogues in Damascus, instructing them to turn over any Christians in their area to Saul so he could bring them bound to Jeruslem (9:1-2). *Jerusalem; 34 A.D.*

***Note:* Saul's Life Before His Conversion**—The book of Acts and the Pauline epistles furnish considerable evidence concerning Saul's early life, as follows:

- Saul was of the house of Israel ("a Jew," Acts 22:3), descended from the tribe of Benjamin, circumcised the eighth day (Philip. 3:5).
- He was born and raised in Tarsus (Acts 21:39, 22:3), a busy metropolis in Cilicia located on the northeast corner of the Mediterranean Sea. He was raised in the city, and most of his metaphors are drawn from city life. His writings reveal an acquaintance with the terminology of Greek philosophy and mystery cults. He must also have been aware of the moral corruption of the city and the idolatrous religions which flourished there.
- He was raised as a faithful Jewish youth, "an Hebrew of the Hebrews" (Philip. 3:5).
- He had a fierce pride in his race, and a strong sense of the promises made to Israel (Rom. 9:3-5; 2 Cor. 11:22).
- He was a Roman citizen (Acts 16:37; 22:25), having inherited his citizenship from his father, for he was "free born" (Acts 22:28).
- He was well educated in the typical Jewish fashion of the day. He learned the Hebrew language (Acts 21:40, 22:2) as well as Aramaic (which he probably spoke at

home), and he knew Greek, his native tongue and the prevalent language of Tarsus. He may also have learned Latin.

● He was well educated in the Jewish scriptures, and would probably have read them from the Greek Septuagint version.

● He learned the trade of tent-making (Acts 18:3).

● He was sent to Jerusalem as a youth (probably at the age of 12), and was raised there. (Acts 22:3).

● He was taught by Gamaliel, a highly regarded rabbi and teacher in Jerusalem, and a member of the Sanhedrin (Acts 22:3). As Paul observed, he was "taught according to the perfect manner of the law of the fathers" (Acts 22:3). His strong rabbinical training was apparent in his frequent appeals to the Old Testament, his use of Midrash legends, his rabbinic exegesis, his apocalyptic expectations, and the unquestioning assumptions in his theology.

● He was "zealous toward God" (Acts 22:3), even more so than others (Gal. 1:14).

● In his zeal he persecuted the Christians, causing many saints to be imprisoned, and bearing testimony which caused them to be put to death (Acts 26:9-11).

● By the time he achieved manhood he was already a leader in the Jewish community in Jerusalem (as evidenced by the authority given him by the high priest (Acts 26:10).

● He was present at the stoning of Stephen, and consented to his death (Acts 22:20).

● An apocryphal source, *Acts of Paul and Thecla,* gives this description of Paul: "He saw Paul coming, a man little of stature, thin-haired upon the head, crooked in the legs, of good state of body, with eyebrows joining, and nose somewhat hooked, full of grace: for sometimes he appeared like a man, and sometimes he had the face of an angel."

56. Saul journeyed to near Damascus. Suddenly the voice of Jesus spoke to him saying, "Saul, Saul, why persecutest thou me?" The voice told Saul to go into the city where he would be told what to do (9:3-7). *The road to Damascus; 34 A.D.* ★

Note: **Three Accounts of Saul's Conversion**—The book of Acts contains three accounts of Saul's conversion: (1) Acts 9:1-18, considered here; (2) Acts 22:3-16, Paul's defense to the citizens of Jerusalem when he had been apprehended by the Romans; and (3) Acts 26:2-18, Paul's discourse to King Agrippa.

57. Saul, left sightless, was led into Damascus where he was three days without sight, food and drink (9:8-9). *Damascus, 34 A.D.*

Note: **Damascus**—In Paul's day Damascus was a busy commercial center, linked to Antioch both politically and economically. It was ruled by Aretas IV from 9 B.C. to 40 A.D. He governed from Petra, capital of his Nabataean kingdom. The city lies east of the Anti-Lebanon mountains and west of the Syrian-Arabian desert, in a beautiful, fertile plain, an oasis in the Arabian desert watered by the Biblical Abana and Parphar rivers. The city was, and still is, famous for its orchards and gardens. Over the centuries it was a communications center, linking the caravan route west to the Mediterranean coast through Tyre to Egypt with the route east across the desert to Assyria and Babylonia. It also was the crossroads for the northern route to Aleppo and the trail south to Arabia. The city is about 180 miles from Jerusalem. Mount Hermon is visible to the southwest and Mount Abana stands on the northwest.

58. The Lord appeared to Ananias in a vision and told Ananias to go and restore Saul's sight, for "he is a chosen vessel unto me, to bear my name before the Gentiles" **(9:10-16).** *Damascus; 34 A.D.* ★

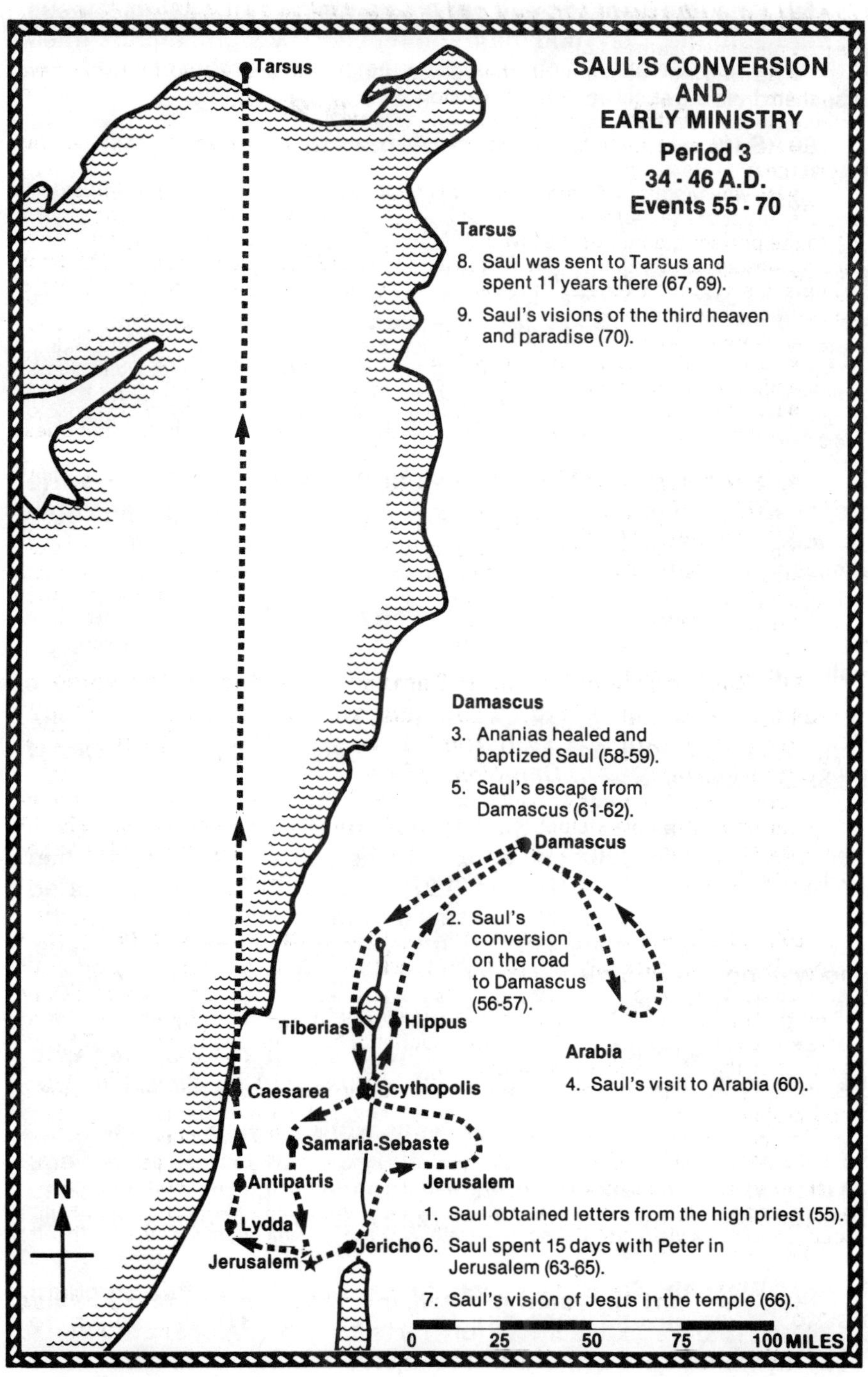
SAUL'S CONVERSION AND EARLY MINISTRY
Period 3
34 - 46 A.D.
Events 55 - 70
Tarsus
8. Saul was sent to Tarsus and spent 11 years there (67, 69).
9. Saul's visions of the third heaven and paradise (70).
Damascus
3. Ananias healed and baptized Saul (58-59).
5. Saul's escape from Damascus (61-62).
Damascus
2. Saul's conversion on the road to Damascus (56-57).
Tiberias
Hippus
Arabia
4. Saul's visit to Arabia (60).
Caesarea
Scythopolis
Samaria-Sebaste
Antipatris
Jerusalem
1. Saul obtained letters from the high priest (55).
Lydda
Jericho
6. Saul spent 15 days with Peter in Jerusalem (63-65).
Jerusalem
7. Saul's vision of Jesus in the temple (66).
Tarsus
N
0
25
50
75
100 MILES

59. Ananias went to Saul, put his hands on him, saying, "Jesus . . . hath sent me, that thou mightest receive thy sight, and be filled with the Holy Ghost." **Saul's sight was immediately restored. He arose and was baptized (9:17-18).** *Damascus; 34 A.D.* ★

60. Saul went to Arabia and returned to Damascus (Gal. 1:13-17). *34 A.D.*

***Note:* The Time of Saul's Sojourn in Arabia**—We learn of this visit to Arabia only in Galatians 1:17. From the context, it appears to have taken place immediately following his conversion, though it may have followed his flight from Damascus three years later (see Gal. 1:18). It is not known exactly where he went, whether it was into the desert for private meditation, or whether he went out to preach. The Arabian desert at that time was part of Nabataea, a kingdom which in this period stretched from the River Euphrates to the Red Sea, with its capital in Petra. Some scholars have conjectured that he went and preached in Nabataea and, while there, somehow incurred the wrath of the Nabataean king, which explains why he had to escape from the local Nabataean governor when he fled by night from Damascus (see 2 Cor. 12:32-33).

61. Saul was with the disciples at Damascus certain days. He preached Christ in the synagogues, increased in strength, and confounded the Jews (9:19-22). *Damascus; 34-36 A.D. Galatians 1:18 seems to indicate that this period lasted for three years.* ★

62. The Jews lay in wait by the city gates to kill Saul, but the disciples helped him to escape by lowering him down the Damascus wall by night in a basket (9:23-25). *36 A.D. (See 2 Cor. 12:32-33.)*

63. Saul came to Jerusalem, but was not accepted by the Christians, who did not believe that he was a disciple of Christ (9:26). *Damascus to Jerusalem; 36 A.D.*

64. Barnabas brought Saul to the apostles and declared unto them how Saul had seen and spoken to the Lord and boldly preached the name of Jesus at Damascus (9:27). (Paul, in Galatians, indicated that the only apostle he actually saw during his visit was Peter, with whom he abode 15 days. He also met James, the brother of Jesus, who was not an apostle but was a leader in the Jerusalem church. See Gal. 1:18-19). *Jerusalem; 15 days, 36 A.D.*

65. Saul spoke boldly in the name of Jesus and disputed with the Grecians at Jerusalem (9:28-29). *Jerusalem; 15 days, 36 A.D.*

66. Saul received a vision of Jesus while praying in the temple. He told Saul, "Make haste, and get thee quickly out of Jerusalem: for they will not receive thy testimony concerning me. . . . I will send thee far hence unto the Gentiles" **(22:17-22).** *Jerusalem; during the 15 days, 36 A.D.* ★

67. When the Grecians sought to slay Saul, the brethren brought him to Caesarea and sent him to Tarsus (9:29-31). *Jerusalem to Tarsus; 36 A.D.*

Note: **Tarsus**—This city was the capital of the Roman province of Cilicia. It is located about ten miles inland from the Mediterranean Sea, about 70 to 80 feet above sea level. It is on a level plain which extends north for about two miles before merging into hills that join the Taurus range about 30 miles further north. The climate is hot and oppressive, so another city was built in the hills. By Roman times the two cities had merged into one and contained a large population. The River Cydnus flows through the city. The ancient river flowed into a lake, which the people engineered and made into a harbor. The city lies on the road to an important mountain pass, the Cilician Gates. Tarsus was an important commercial center, and also a center of learning with a university.

68. Persecution against the church in Judea, Samaria and Galilee ended. The church was edified and multiplied (9:31). *Throughout northern Palestine; 36-44 A.D.* ★

69. Saul's "hidden years" in Tarsus: The Bible tells almost nothing of Saul's activities for a seven-year period, from 36-43 A.D., nor are we aware of the exact length of this interval. Presumably he was actively engaged in missionary work among the Gentiles of Cilicia and Syria during that time. Many of the trials Paul wrote about in 2 Corinthians 11:23-27 probably occurred during this time: beatings with 39 stripes five times; once stoned; three times shipwrecked; many journeys with perils from robbers, Jews and heathens; weariness, pain, hunger and thirst, cold and nakedness.

70. Saul's vision of the third heaven and of Paradise, recorded in 2 Corinthians 12:1-4, must have been given to him during this period also. (If 2 Corinthians was written in 56 A.D., and these visions were received 14 years previous, the date would have been about 42 or 43 A.D.) ★

ROMAN PROCURATORS OF JUDAEA AND PALESTINE

In Roman government, there were two types of provinces: public provinces governed by the Senate, and imperial provinces governed by the Emperor. The Senate governed those which were peaceful and did not require the presence of an army. The Emperor controlled the disturbed provinces where armed forces were required to maintain peace. Judea became a province in A.D. 6, and was under the authority of the Roman emperor. Less important provinces such as Judaea were governed by a *procurator*, a man of equestrian rank whose main duty was to procure revenue for the Romans. He was a civil official, not a military officer (though he sometimes commanded an auxiliary military contingent, but not Roman legionaires) and was chosen for his financial abilities rather than his ability to govern equitably.

Coponius, A.D. 6-9
M. Ambivius, A.D. 9-12
Annius Rufus, A.D. 12-15
Valerius Gratus, A.D. 15-26
Pontius Pilate, A.D. 26-36
Marcellus, A.D. 36-37
Marullus, A.D. 37?
Herennius Capito, A.D. 37-41
Cuspius Fadus, A.D. 44-46
Tiberius Julius Alexander, A.D. 46-48
Ventidius Cumanus, A.D. 48-52
Antonius Felix, A.D. 52-60
Porcius Festus, A.D. 60-62?
Clodius Albinus, A.D. 62-64
Gessius Florus, A.D. 64-66

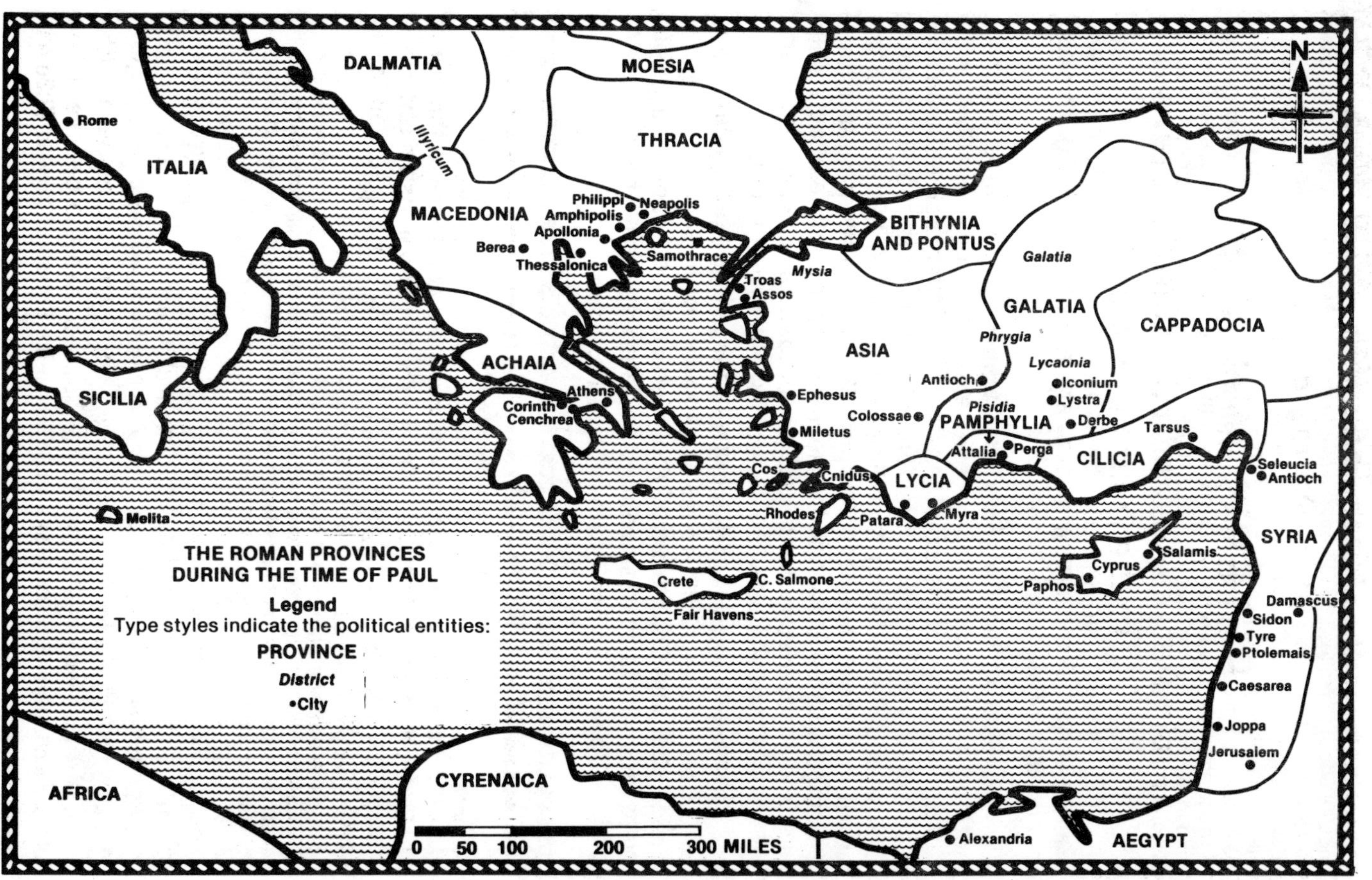

THE ROMAN PROVINCES
DURING THE TIME OF PAUL
Legend
Type styles indicate the political entities:
PROVINCE
District
•City
N
0 50 100 200 300 MILES
DALMATIA
MOESIA
THRACIA
Illyricum
ITALIA
Rome
MACEDONIA
Philippi
Neapolis
Amphipolis
Apollonia
Berea
Thessalonica
Samothrace
BITHYNIA
AND PONTUS
Galatia
GALATIA
CAPPADOCIA
Troas
Assos
Mysia
ASIA
Phrygia
Lycaonia
Antioch
Iconium
Lystra
Pisidia
PAMPHYLIA
Derbe
Tarsus
CILICIA
Attalia
Perga
SICILIA
ACHAIA
Athens
Corinth
Cenchrea
Ephesus
Colossae
Miletus
Cos
Cnidus
LYCIA
Rhodes
Patara
Myra
Seleucia
Antioch
SYRIA
Melita
Salamis
Cyprus
Paphos
Crete
C. Salmone
Fair Havens
Damascus
Sidon
Tyre
Ptolemais
Caesarea
Joppa
Jerusalem
AFRICA
CYRENAICA
Alexandria
AEGYPT

Period 4

PETER'S MINISTRY

(From Peter's Visits to the Coastal Cities to the Death of Herod)

43 A.D. to 47 A.D.

Acts 9:31 to 12:24

Peter Heals Aeneas and Tabitha
Peter's Vision of the Unclean Animals
Peter Begins Preaching to the Gentiles
Peter Baptizes the Household of Cornelius
The Gospel Is Carried to Phoenicia, Cyprus, and Antioch
Barnabas Brings Saul to Antioch For a Year
The Disciples Are Called Christians at Antioch
Barnabas and Saul Bring Food to the Saints at Jerusalem
Herod Kills the Apostle John
Peter Is Released From Prison by an Angel
Peter Moves to Caesarea
The Death of Herod Agrippa I
The Book of James Is Written

71. Peter passed throughout all quarters, and came to the saints at Lydda. He healed Aeneas there, who had been in bed eight years with palsy. The saints at Lydda and Saron saw him and turned to the Lord (9:32-35). *Throughout Judea, to Lydda; 43 A.D.* ★

Note: **Lydda and the Plain of Sharon**—Lydda, also known as Lod, was located in the plain of Sharon on the great caravan route between Egypt and Babylon. The village was about 10 miles southeast of Joppa, on a road which led to Jerusalem. It lay in a river valley in a hollow of the hills. The village was built by people of the tribe of Benjamin in the period shortly after the promised land was occupied by the Israelites. Saron, better known as Sharon, is the fruitful seacoast plain extending from Carmel to Joppa along the shores of the Mediterranean.

72. Tabitha (Dorcas), a disciple at Joppa, became sick and died. The disciples sent for Peter at Lydda. Peter came and called Tabitha back to life. Her restoration to life caused many to believe in the Lord. Peter tarried many days in Joppa with Simon, a tanner (9:36-43). *Lydda to Joppa; 43 A.D.* ★

Note: **Joppa**—The city (modern-day Jaffa) was Israel's principal seaport in southern Palestine on the Mediterranean. It is the only elevation between Caesarea and Gaza along the low coastline. Its harbor and direct road to Jerusalem made it one of the most important cities along the coast. A rocky hill separated houses along the coast from a fertile area of palm and fruit trees inland from the city.

73. Cornelius, a Roman centurion living in Caesarea and a devout man, saw an angel in a vision. The angel told him "Thy prayers and thine alms are come up for a memorial before God," **and told him to send men to Joppa to summon Peter (10:1-8).** *Caesarea; 43 A.D.* ★

Note: **Caesarea**—This city was rebuilt by Herod the Great on the site of Straton's Tower. It was completed about 9 B.C. after ten years of construction. It was elaborately constructed, with a large harbor, a hippodrome, a 20,000-seat ampitheater, a theater, a court of justice, two aqueducts, a large surrounding wall, and many statues. The city was the site of lavish games and entertainments. It became the official residence for the Roman procurators of Palestine. After Jerusalem was destroyed by Titus and his Roman army in 70 A.D., Rome made Caesarea the capital of Palestine.

Note: **Roman Army Organization**—The Roman army was divided into several levels. A legion, consisting of about 6,000 men, was divided into 10 cohorts, each commanded by a tribune. A cohort was divided into six centuries, each commanded by a centurion. A centurion, then, was a commander of 100 men. Centurions were usually men of good character and leadership ability who had risen from the ranks. Cornelius' century was recruited in Italy and was made up primarily of men who were Roman citizens. Thus they were called the "Italian band."

74. Peter received a vision in which he was commanded to eat animals which were unclean according to Mosaic law. He refused, saying he had never eaten anything that was common or unclean. He was told, "What God has cleansed, that call not thou common" **(10:9-16).** *Joppa, at Simon's house by the seaside; 43 A.D.* ★

Note: **Prayer On the Housetop**—The flat housetops were used for prayer and meditation, as well as for sleeping and recreation. They provided a pleasant, private place with cool breezes for comfort. Peter's prayer was offered at the sixth hour, or noon.

75. When the men from Cornelius came to Simon's home, the Spirit told Peter, "Get thee down, and go with them, doubting nothing." **Peter and other brethren from Joppa accompanied the men to Caesarea (10:17-23).** *Joppa to Caesarea (about 40 miles); 43 A.D.* ★

76. Peter came to the house of Cornelius and found the centurion had assembled his family and friends. Cornelius told Peter of the vision in which he was told to summon the apostle. Peter responded, "Of a truth I perceive that God is no respecter of persons," **and preached to him of Christ (10:24-43).** *Caesarea, at the home of Cornelius; 43 A.D.* ***[★ —Major Discourse #4]***

77. The Holy Ghost fell on those who heard Peter's words. They spoke with tongues and magnified God. Peter commanded them to be baptized in the name of the Lord (10:44-48). *Caesarea; 43 A.D.* ★

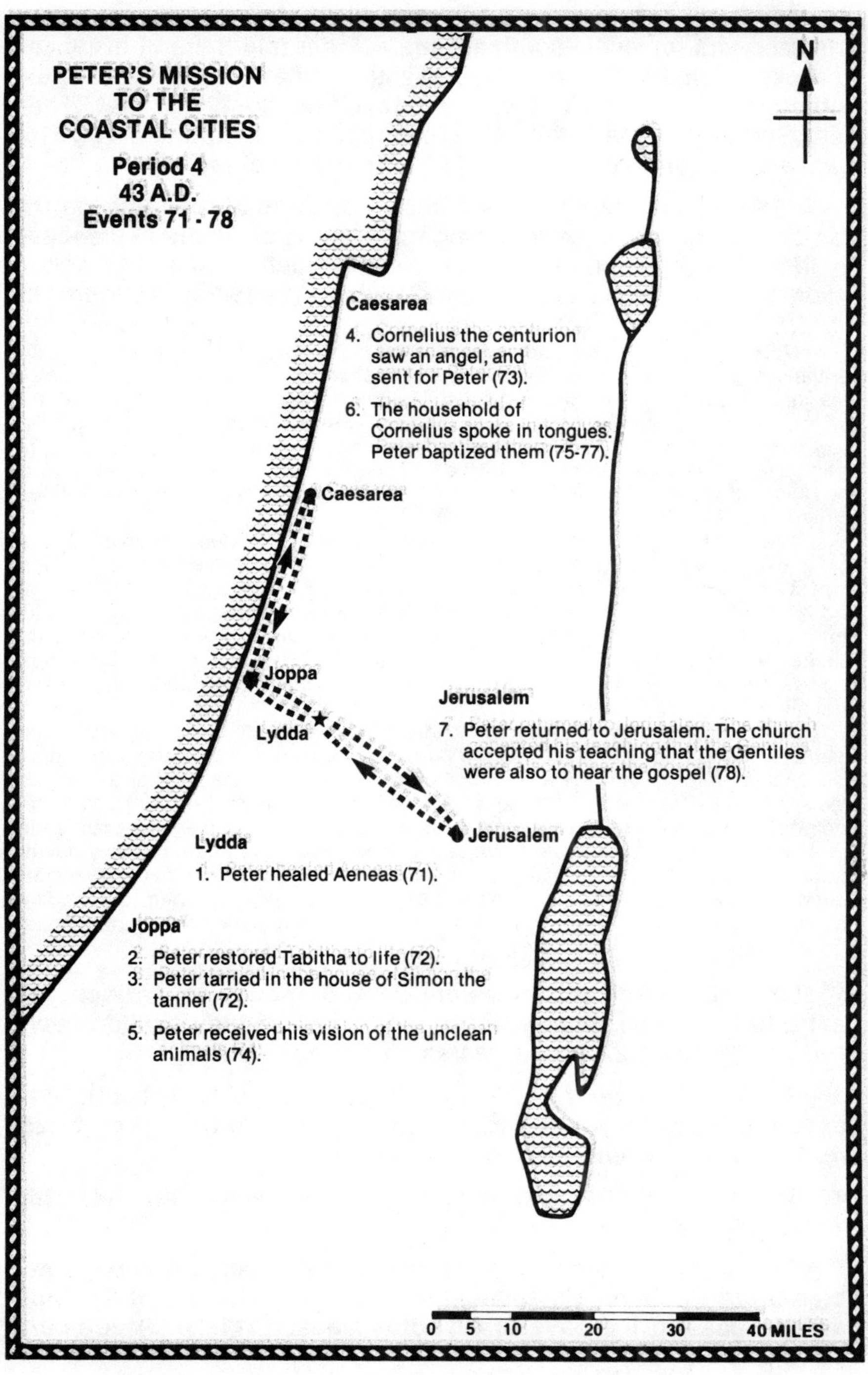

PETER'S MISSION TO THE COASTAL CITIES
Period 4
43 A.D.
Events 71 - 78
N
Caesarea
4. Cornelius the centurion saw an angel, and sent for Peter (73).
6. The household of Cornelius spoke in tongues. Peter baptized them (75-77).
Caesarea
Joppa
Lydda
Jerusalem
7. Peter returned to Jerusalem. The church accepted his teaching that the Gentiles were also to hear the gospel (78).
Jerusalem
Lydda
1. Peter healed Aeneas (71).
Joppa
2. Peter restored Tabitha to life (72).
3. Peter tarried in the house of Simon the tanner (72).
5. Peter received his vision of the unclean animals (74).
0 5 10 20 30 40 MILES

78. Peter returned to Jerusalem. The circumcised members criticized him for visiting with a Gentile. Peter told them of his vision and experience with Cornelius, saying, "What was I, that I could withstand God?" **They accepted his teaching, observing that** "Then hath God also to the Gentiles granted repentance unto life" **(11:1-18).** *Caesarea to Jerusalem; 43 A.D.* ***[★ —Major Discourse #5]***

79. The members who had been scattered abroad (during the persecution which arose following the stoning of Stephen) preached to the Jews in Phenice, Cyprus, and Antioch. Those in Antioch made many converts among the Grecians (11:19-21). *Antioch; 35-44 A.D.*

Note: **Phenice, Cyprus and Antioch**—*Phoenicia* (Phenice) was the Greek term for the country on the coast of Syria (modern Lebanon). The native name for Phoenicia was *Kenaan* (Canaan), meaning "lowland," as contrasted with the adjoining *Aram*, or highland (the Hebrew name for Syria). The area was a coastal plain about 28 miles long, with a width of 2 to 5 miles between the sea and the mountains to the east. The Greek name *Phoenicia* meant "palm tree." At the time of Paul, the area was part of the Roman province of Syria, so its inhabitants were, at the same time, Canaanites, Syrians and Phoenicians.

The isle of *Cyprus*, in the northeastern corner of the Mediterannean Sea, is about 40 miles west of the Syrian coast and 60 miles south of Turkey. It is the third-largest island in the Mediterranean, with 3,572 square miles (about 140 miles long and 60 miles wide) and 486 miles of coast. It has long been regarded as politically significant because of its strategic importance for political and military control of the Middle East and because of its natural resources, particularly copper. The most important mercantile city was Salamis, while Paphos was the capital of the island. That city housed the Roman garrison.

Antioch (called Syrian Antioch to distinguish it from the other Antioch in Pisidia) was the third largest city in the Roman empire (after Rome and Alexandria). It is located on the Orontes River, about 15 miles inland from the Mediterranean, and was serviced by the nearby port city of Seleucia. It was a busy center of commerce and government, for it lay on the main trade route between Rome and Mesopotamia. It was also a pleasure center, and housed a large heathen temple. In Paul's day its population was more than 500,000. It was the capital of the province of Syria, and the seat of the Roman governor. Though most of its population was Syrian, its language and culture were Greek. There was also a large Jewish population there, which made it an attractive prospect for proselyting.

80. The church at Jerusalem sent Barnabas to Antioch. He "exhorted them all, that with purpose of heart they would cleave unto the Lord" **(11:22-24).** *Jerusalem to Antioch; 42 A.D.*

81. Barnabas went to Tarsus and brought Saul to Antioch. They associated with the church there and taught them for a year (11:25-26). *Antioch to Tarsus to Antioch; 42-43 A.D.*

82. The disciples were called Christians first in Antioch (11:26). *Antioch; 44 A.D.*

83. Prophets from Jerusalem came to Antioch. Agabus prophecied there would be a great dearth throughout all the world (which came to pass in the days of Claudius Caesar) (11:27-28). *Antioch; 44 A.D.*

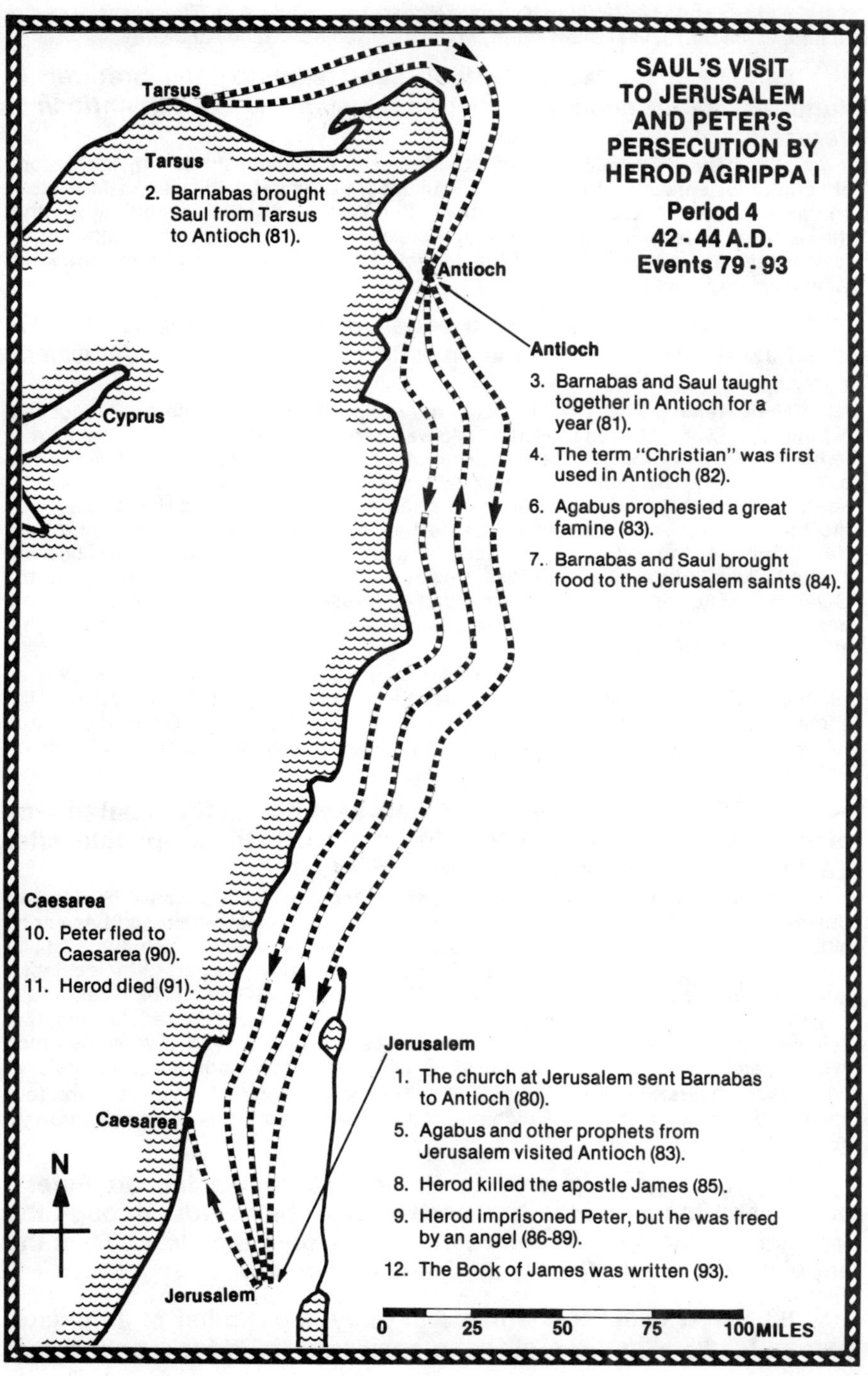
SAUL'S VISIT
TO JERUSALEM
AND PETER'S
PERSECUTION BY
HEROD AGRIPPA I
Period 4
42 - 44 A.D.
Events 79 - 93
Tarsus
Tarsus
2. Barnabas brought Saul from Tarsus to Antioch (81).
Antioch
Antioch
3. Barnabas and Saul taught together in Antioch for a year (81).
4. The term "Christian" was first used in Antioch (82).
6. Agabus prophesied a great famine (83).
7.. Barnabas and Saul brought food to the Jerusalem saints (84).
Cyprus
Caesarea
10. Peter fled to Caesarea (90).
11. Herod died (91).
Jerusalem
1. The church at Jerusalem sent Barnabas to Antioch (80).
5. Agabus and other prophets from Jerusalem visited Antioch (83).
8. Herod killed the apostle James (85).
9. Herod imprisoned Peter, but he was freed by an angel (86-89).
12. The Book of James was written (93).
Caesarea
N
Jerusalem
0
25
50
75
100 MILES

Note: **Famine**—Claudius Caesar reigned from 41-54 A.D. There was a severe famine in the fourth year of his reign, which affected both Judea and Greece.

84. The disciples at Antioch sent relief to their brethren in Judea. Barnabas and Saul took it to the elders (11:29-30). *Antioch to Jerusalem; 44 A.D.*

Note: **The Visit to Jerusalem Mentioned in Galatians 2:1-10**—In the second chapter of his epistle to the Galatians, Paul described in detail his visit to Jerusalem, and a subsequent visit by Peter to Antioch. Scholars are divided concerning whether the verses in Galatians refer to this visit (Acts 11:29-30) or to Paul's visit following his first missionary journey to attend the council at Jerusalem (Acts 15:1-31). The latter view is more generally accepted.

85. Herod the King vexed certain members of the church. He killed James, the brother of John, with the sword (12:1-2). *Jerusalem; early spring, 44 A.D.*

Note: **Herod the King**—This was Herod Agrippa I, son of Bernice and Aristobulus (who was the son of Herod the Great). He was born in 10 B.C., and ruled from 37 A.D. to his death in 44 A.D. The territory previously governed by the house of Herod had been taken away by Rome, but in 37 A.D. the emperor Caligula began to give the northern areas back to Herod Agrippa I to rule. Caligula also allowed Herod to assume the title of king. When Claudius became the Roman emperor in 41 A.D., he gave Herod Agrippa I the southern areas of Judea and Samaria, so Herod Agrippa I became king and ruler over all the territories previously ruled by his grandfather, Herod the Great. Herod Agrippa I left Rome and came to Jerusalem, where he ruled and did his best to appear to be an orthodox Jew. His persecution of the church was part of his effort to maintain that image.

Note: **The Death of James**—This was the apostle James, also known as "James the Great." He was the son of Zebedee and Salome, and elder brother of the apostle John. These two brothers, along with Peter, were the leaders of the church following the ascension of the Savior. It is believed that he was beheaded by Herod Agrippa.

86. Herod imprisoned Peter, delivered him to four quaternions of soldiers, and intended to bring him forth to the people after Easter (12:3-4). *Jerusalem; early spring, 44 A.D.*

Note: **The Days of Unleavened Bread, the Passover, and Easter**—The Feast of Unleavened Bread and the Passover were two separate feasts which had been combined into one by New Testament times. The commandment in Exodus 12:14-17 called for the people to eat unleavened bread for seven days, as part of their celebration of having been led by the Lord out of Egypt. (See also Deut. 16:1-8, Ezek. 45:21-24.) This passage is the only place in the Bible where the term "Easter" is used. It is believed that it found its way into the King James version from earlier versions which avoided, as much as possible, expressions which the people could not understand.

Note: **Quaternion of Soldiers**—The four quaternions of soldiers were four squads of four soldiers each, which relieved each other at regular intervals throughout the night.

87. An angel appeared to Peter. The chains fell off Peter's hands, and the angel led him unseen past the guards, through the iron gate which opened of its own accord, onto the street. Then the angel disappeared (12:5-11). *Jerusalem; April, 44 A.D.* ★

88. Peter came to the home of Mary, the mother of John (surnamed Mark). When the girl who answered the door reported that

Peter was there, they thought he was dead, and said "It is his angel." **When they came to the door, Peter told them how he escaped and sent word to the brethren (12:12-17).** *Jerusalem; April, 44 A.D.* ★

Note: **The Home of Mary**—Mary was the mother of Mark (author of the gospel of Mark) and an aunt of Barnabas. She was a widow and was wealthy. Members of the church would gather in her home to worship. Many believe that her home was the location of the Savior's last supper and the place where the Holy Ghost descended upon the saints on the Day of Pentecost.

89. Herod put the keepers who were supposed to be guarding Peter to death (12:18-19). *Jerusalem; April, 44 A.D.*

90. Peter went from Judea to Caesarea and abode there (12:19). *Jerusalem to Caesarea; April, 44 A.D.*

91. Herod made an oration to visitors from Tyre and Sidon. When the people shouted that it was the voice of God and not of man, and he failed to give God the glory, the angel of the Lord smote him. He was eaten of worms, and he died (12:20-23). *Caesarea; spring 44 A.D.* ★

Note: **Josephus' Account of Herod's Death**—The great historian, Josephus (in his *Antiquities of the Jews,* XIX, viii, 2) gives details concerning this event. He recorded that it took place in Caesarea, on the second day of a festival. Herod wore a garment made out of silver. The rays of the early morning sun made his clothing shine, till the people believed that he was a god. He recorded that Herod was stricken with great pain at the festival and died five days later.

92. The word of God grew and multiplied (12:24). *Throughout Palestine; 44-47 A.D.*

93. The book of James was written. *Jerusalem(?); 45-46 A.D.*

Note: **The Book of James**—Though the matter is uncertain, ecclesiastical tradition has held since the third century that the author of this epistle was James, the brother of Jesus, rather than one of the two James who were apostles (James the Great, the brother of John; or James the lesser, son of Alphaeus and Mary and brother of Matthew). The gospel of Mark speaks of James as a brother of Jesus (Mark 6:3), as does Matthew (Matt. 13:55). (See also John 2:12; 7:3, 10.)

ROMAN LEGATES IN PALESTINE

In Roman government, a *legate* was a governor of a province who had greater power than a *procurator.* Legates held senatorial rank, and had a strong force of Roman legionaires under their command. They were usually chosen from the aristocracy. Legates ruled in the province of Syria beginning in 57 B.C., but the first legate in Palestine was Vespasian, beginning in A.D. 67.

Vespasian, A.D. 67-69
Titus, A.D. 70
Sextus Vettulenus Cerealis, A.D. 70
Lucilius Bassus, A.D. 71
L. Flavius Silva, A.D. 72-80?
M. Salvidenus, A.D. 80-85
Cn. Pompeius Longinus, A.D. 86-?
Atticus, ca. A.D. 107
Pompeius Falco, ca. A.D. 107-114
Tiberianus, ca. A.D. 114-117
Lusius Quietus, ca. A.D. 117-?
Tineius Rufus, A.D. 132-135
Julius Severus, A.D. 135

THE KINGDOM OF HEROD AGRIPPA I
37 - 44 A.D.
Agrippa I was the grandson of King Herod the Great, and the son of Aristobulus. He became a favorite of the Roman emperors Caligula and Claudius, who gave him these lands to rule. As a youth, he first ruled only the tiny area of Chalcis, but additional responsibility was placed upon him as he matured. In 37 A.D. he was given Philip's tetrarchy. He received Antipus' tetrarchy in 39 A.D. Lands formerly ruled by Archelaus were awarded to him in 41 A.D. Thus he united almost all of his grandfather's kingdom under his power.
N
Chalcis
Abila
SYRIA
Sidon
PHOENICIA
Damascus
Tyre
Caesarea Philippi
GAULANITIS
TRACHONITIS
Ptolemais
GALILEE
BATANEA
Naveh
Gamala
Canatha
Tiberias
Sepphoris
Hippus
AURANITIS
Mediterranean Sea
Dora
Gadara
Scythopolis
Caesarea
Pella
DECAPOLIS
Sebaste
SAMARIA
Antipatris
River Jordan
Joppa
Gadora
PEREA
Philadelphia
Jamnia
Jericho
Azotus
Jerusalem
Ascalon
NABATEANS
JUDAEA
Gaza
Dead Sea
Caligula's grant—37 A.D.
Caligula's grant—39 A.D.
Claudius' grant—39 A.D.
Kingdom of Herod of Chalcis.
Agrippa I's kingdom—44 A.D.
0 10 20 30 MILES

Period 5

PAUL'S FIRST MISSIONARY JOURNEY

(The First Missionary Journey Lasted About 18 Months)

45 A.D. to 48 A.D.

Acts 12:25 to 14:28

Saul Labors in Antioch for Two Years
Barnabas, Saul and Mark Depart to Preach
Saul Preaches to Sergius Paulus, Roman Governor of Cyprus
Saul Rebukes and Blinds Elymas the Sorcerer
Saul Becomes Known as Paul
Paul's Discourse in the Antioch Synagogue
Paul and Barnabas Turn to the Gentiles
Paul Heals a Crippled Man at Lystra
The People at Lystra Believe Paul and Barnabas are Gods
Paul is Stoned at Lystra
Elders Are Ordained in Every Church

94. Barnabas and Saul returned from Jerusalem to Antioch, and took John Mark with them (12:25). *Jerusalem to Antioch; 44 A.D.*

Note: **John Mark**—John, surnamed Mark (Acts 12:25), was a Jew, the son of a widow named Mary who owned a large home in Jerusalem which was a gathering place for members of the early church (Acts 12:12). He was a cousin to Barnabas (Col. 4:10). The surname Mark was probably an added name which his family took in Roman fashion. This custom was popular among Greek-speaking people, though less common among the Jews. Mark went with Barnabas and Saul to Antioch, and then accompanied them on their first missionary journey, though he left them in Perga of Pamphylia to return to Jerusalem (Acts 13:13). Mark also went with Barnabas on his second missionary journey to Cyprus (Acts 15:37-39). In later years he was with Timothy at Ephesus (2 Tim. 4:11), then with Paul at Rome (Col. 4:10; Philem. 24), and also with Peter at Rome (1 Pet. 5:13), where he wrote his gospel under Peter's direction for the use of the church at Rome. According to tradition, Mark visited Egypt after the death of Peter. There he founded the church at Alexandria, and eventually was martyred there.

95. Saul labored in Antioch for about two years. *Antioch; 45-46 A.D.*

96. The Holy Ghost told the prophets and teachers in Antioch (Barnabas, Simeon, Lucius, Manaen, and Saul): "Separate me Barnabas and Saul for the work whereunto I have called them" **(13:1-2).** *Antioch; 47 A.D.* ★

97. The prophets and teachers fasted and prayed, laid their hands on them, and sent them away (13:3). *Antioch; 47 A.D.* ★

98. Barnabas, Saul and Mark departed unto Seleucia, and sailed from there to Cyprus (13:4). *Antioch to Cyprus; 47 A.D.*

Note: **Seleucia**—This city was on the coast of Syria, above the mouth of the Orontes River. Founded by Seleucus I (who planned to use it as his capital, though he shifted his capital to Antioch because he could not control the sea), it was an important fortress city that played a significant role in various wars for several hundred years before the time of Paul. Pompey declared it a free city, and it was a major trade city and outlet to the sea for Antioch in Paul's day. The city was sometimes called Seleucia Pieria, after a mountain to its north, to distinguish it from other cities of the same name.

99. Barnabas and Saul preached in the Jewish synagogues at Salamis, with the help of John Mark (13:5). *Salamis, on the isle of Cyprus; 47 A.D.*

Note: **Salamis**—This seaport city, on the east side of the island of Cyprus, was a flourishing Greek seaport with a significant Syrian trade in Paul's day. It was the government seat for the eastern side of the island. Many Jews had settled there, and it was a fertile field for missionary labor. In 116-117 A.D., during the reign of Trajan, the Jews rose up and destroyed the city. As a result, the Jewish population was annihilated, and Jews were not allowed on the island from that time forward. The harbor eventually became filled with silt and the city is now deserted.

100. When they went through the isle to Paphos, Sergius Paulus, the deputy of the country, called for them and desired to hear the word of God (13:6-7). *Salamis to Paphos, on the isle of Cyprus; 47 A.D.*

Note: **Paphos**—New Paphos (modern Baffo) was the second of two cities known by that name on the isle of Cyprus. It was the center for the Roman government on the island. Cyprus was annexed by the Romans in 55 B.C., and became a Senatorial province in 22 B.C., with a governor bearing the title of proconsul. In Saul's day the port, located on the west side of the island, was a Roman naval station.

Note: **Sergius Paulus**—He was the Roman proconsul, or governor of the isle of Cyprus in Saul's day. Saul's preaching of the gospel to him was the first known presentation of Christianity before a Roman civil authority.

101. Elymas the sorcerer (a Jewish false prophet named Barjesus) withstood Barnabas and Saul, seeking to turn away the Roman deputy Sergius Paulus from the Christian faith. Saul rebuked him, saying: "Wilt thou not cease to pervert the right ways of the Lord?" **Saul cursed him with temporary blindness and Elymas immediately became blind. The deputy believed (13:8-12).** *Paphos, on the isle of Cyprus; 47 A.D.* ★

102. Saul is referred to as Paul for the first time (13:9). *Paphos, on the isle of Cyprus; 47 A.D.*

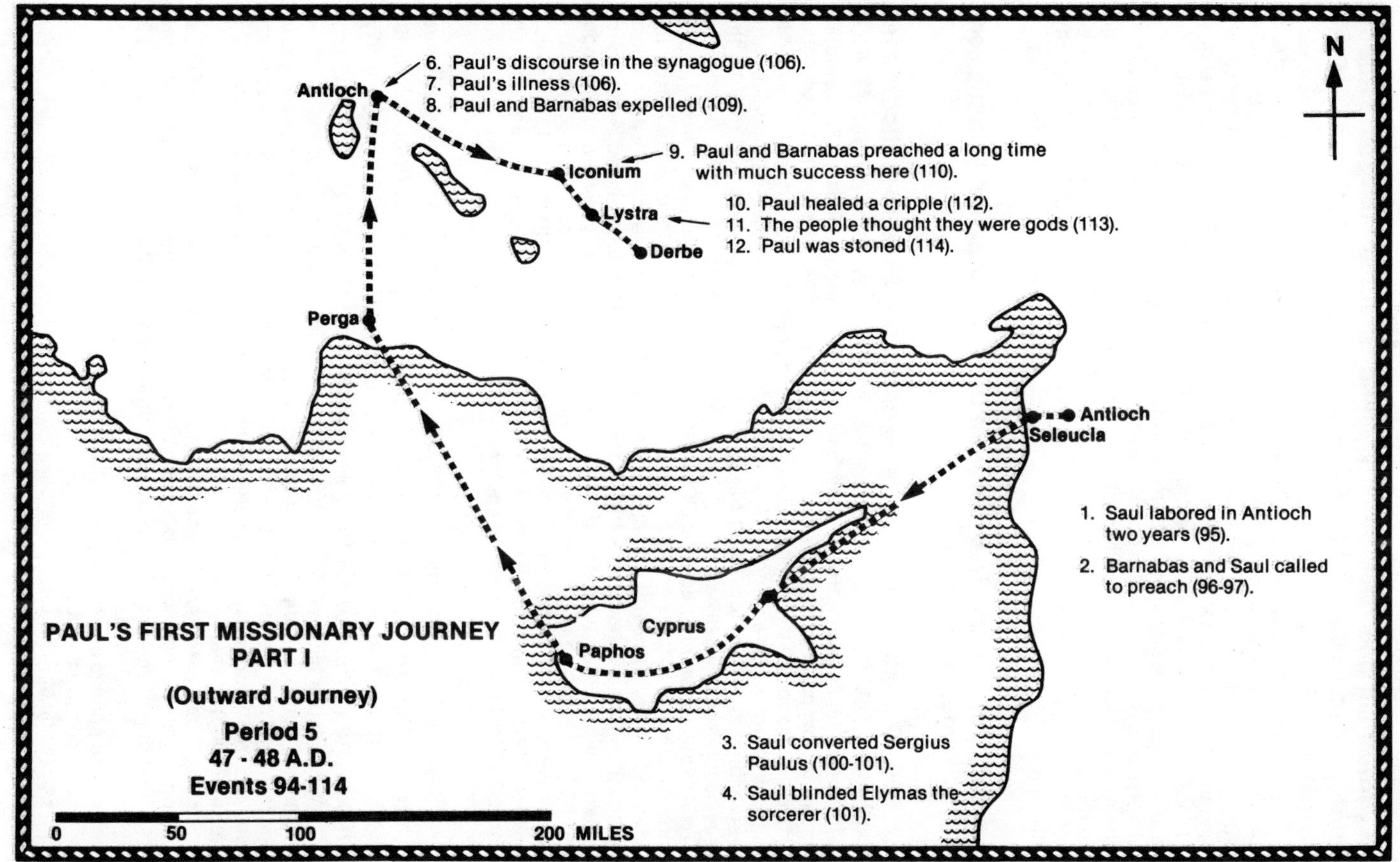
N
Antioch
6. Paul's discourse in the synagogue (106).
7. Paul's illness (106).
8. Paul and Barnabas expelled (109).
9. Paul and Barnabas preached a long time with much success here (110).
Iconium
Lystra
Derbe
10. Paul healed a cripple (112).
11. The people thought they were gods (113).
12. Paul was stoned (114).
Perga
Antioch
Seleucia
1. Saul labored in Antioch two years (95).
2. Barnabas and Saul called to preach (96-97).
Cyprus
Paphos
PAUL'S FIRST MISSIONARY JOURNEY
PART I
(Outward Journey)
Period 5
47 - 48 A.D.
Events 94-114
3. Saul converted Sergius Paulus (100-101).
4. Saul blinded Elymas the sorcerer (101).
0
50
100
200 MILES

103. Paul and his company sailed from Paphos, and came to Perga in Pamphylia (13:13). *Paphos, on Cyprus, to Perga in Pamphylilia; 47 A.D.*

Note: **Pamphylia and Perga**—Pamphylia was a Roman district on the southern coast of Asia Minor, situated between the districts of Lycia and Cilicia. It was an 80-mile-long plain, 20 miles wide at its broadest point, sandwiched between Mt. Taurus and the Mediterranean Sea. The area was isolated from inland travel because of a lack of good roads, and the best access was from the sea. The low land was very malarious, and never became the base for a major population.

Perga and **Attalia** were major cities of the province. Attalia was located on the edge of the plain, built in a crescent around a beautiful natural harbor. Perga was situated 8 miles inland but was still a seaport because it was located on a navigable river, the Cestrus River. The city had a 160-foot-high acropolis, a walled lower city, and a citadel.

104. John (Mark) departed from them and returned to Jerusalem (13:13). *Perga, in Pamphylia; 47 A.D.*

105. Barnabas and Paul left Perga and came to Antioch near Pisidia (13:14). *Perga, in Pamphylia, to Antioch, in Phrygia; 47 A.D.*

Note: **Pisidia and Antioch**—Pisidia was a Roman district located in the mountainous region north of the coastal district of Pamphylia. The district was about 50 miles wide and 120 miles long. It is an area composed almost entirely of mountain ranges with deep intersecting valleys. In Paul's day it was a dangerous place, with few inhabitants except for roving bands of thieves and brigands, and may be the place he referred to when he wrote of "perils from robbers" (2 Cor. 11:26).

Antioch (often referred to as "Pisidian Antioch" to distinguish it from the city of the same name in Syria ("Syrian Antioch"), really wasn't in Pisidia, but across the undefined border in nearby Phrygia, an ethnic district in the Roman province of Galatia. The Romans made it a free town, and Augustus established a colony of soldiers there to keep the brigands and barbarians of the neighboring areas under control. The language spoken in the city was Latin and the municipal government was modeled after Roman municipalities. The city was on the major route which connected Syria with Ephesus, so it was a city which held both civil and military importance for the entire region of southern Galatia.

106. Paul's discourse about Jesus in the synagogue at Antioch: "Through this man is preached unto you the forgiveness of sins: And by him all that believe are justified from all things" **(13:14-41).** *Antioch, near Pisidia; 47 A.D.* ***[★ —Major Discourse #6]***

Note: **Paul's Illness**—The Epistle to the Galatians (addressed to the saints in the cities of Antioch, Iconium, Lystra, and Derbe), indicates that Paul preached to them through "infirmity of the flesh" on his first visit there (Gal. 4:13). Some scholars have theorized that he caught malaria in the low-lying Perga area, and came to the cities in the higher areas to try to overcome it.

Note: **The Synagogue Service**—In those days, as in modern times, the typical synagogue service on the Jewish Sabbath consisted of the following elements:

- Reciting of the Shema (the Jewish confession of faith) found in Deut. 6:4-9, 11:13-21, and Num. 15:37-41.
- Fixed prayers and benedictions.
- A lesson from the Law.
- A sermon or instructional period.

The ruler of the synagogue would decide who was to read or preach.

107. The Gentiles asked Paul and Barnabas to preach to them the next Sabbath. When almost the whole city came to hear them, the Jews were filled with envy, and spake against the things spoken by Paul, contradicting him (13:42-45). *Antioch, near Pisidia; a week later on the Sabbath; 47 A.D.*

108. Paul and Barnabas rebuked the Jews, saying: "We turn to the Gentiles." **The word of the Lord was published throughout all the region (13:46-49).** *Region around Antioch; 47 A.D.* ★

109. The Jews stirred up persecution against Paul and Barnabas and expelled them. They came to Iconium (13:50-52). *Antioch to Iconium; 47 A.D.*

110. In Iconium many Jews and Greeks believed, and Paul and Barnabas abode a long time speaking boldly in the Lord. But unbelieving Jews stirred up the Gentiles, which divided the city. The Jews plotted to attack and stone them (14:1-5). *Iconium; 47-48 A.D.* ★

Note: **Iconium**—This was the easternmost city of the district of Phrygia, near the border of Lycaonia, about 80 miles southeast of Antioch. The city, now named Konia, has been a large and busy site from Biblical times to the present. It is situated at the western edge of the Asia Minor's vast central plain, it is well watered and surrounded by beautiful orchards. It was 18 miles away from Lystra, and a direct route joined them. This city was an important center of Christian life for many centuries.

Note: **"The Acts of Paul and Thecla"**—This romance, written in the second century, furnishes numerous details of Paul's activities in Iconium, some of which scholars feel may be authentic.

111. Paul and Barnabas fled to Lystra and Derbe, cities of Lycaonia, and preached in that region (14:6-7). *Iconium to Lystra and Derbe; 48 A.D.*

Note: **Lycaonia, Lystra and Derbe**—Lycaonia was a district which had undergone many boundary changes over the centuries, with its cities being assigned to Galatia and Cappadocia at different periods. The area is ideal pasture land, a level plain which merges on the north and east with the plains of Galatia and Cappadocia, and on the south and west by hilly regions.

Lystra was a small town in Lycaonia which the Romans made a colony on the imperial road to Antioch. It was an area relatively untouched by Hellinization, and the city does not exist today. Timothy was a native of Lystra (Acts 16:1-5), and the missionaries may have lodged with his mother, Eunice, and grandmother, Lois, there (2 Tim. 1:5).

Derbe was also a small town in Lycaonia. It lay on the road from the Cilician Gates to Lystra and Iconium, about 30 miles southeast of Lystra. The Lycaonian tongue was spoken in these towns (Acts 14:11). Paul's helper Gaius was from Derbe (Acts 20:4).

112. Paul healed a crippled man, who had faith to be healed, at Lystra (14:8-10). *Lystra; 48 A.D.* ★

113. The people, believing the missionaries were gods, called Barnabas Jupiter and Paul Mercurius. The apostles restrained the people from offering sacrifices to them, saying: "Ye should turn from these vanities unto the living God" **(14:11-18).** *Lystra; 48 A.D.* ★

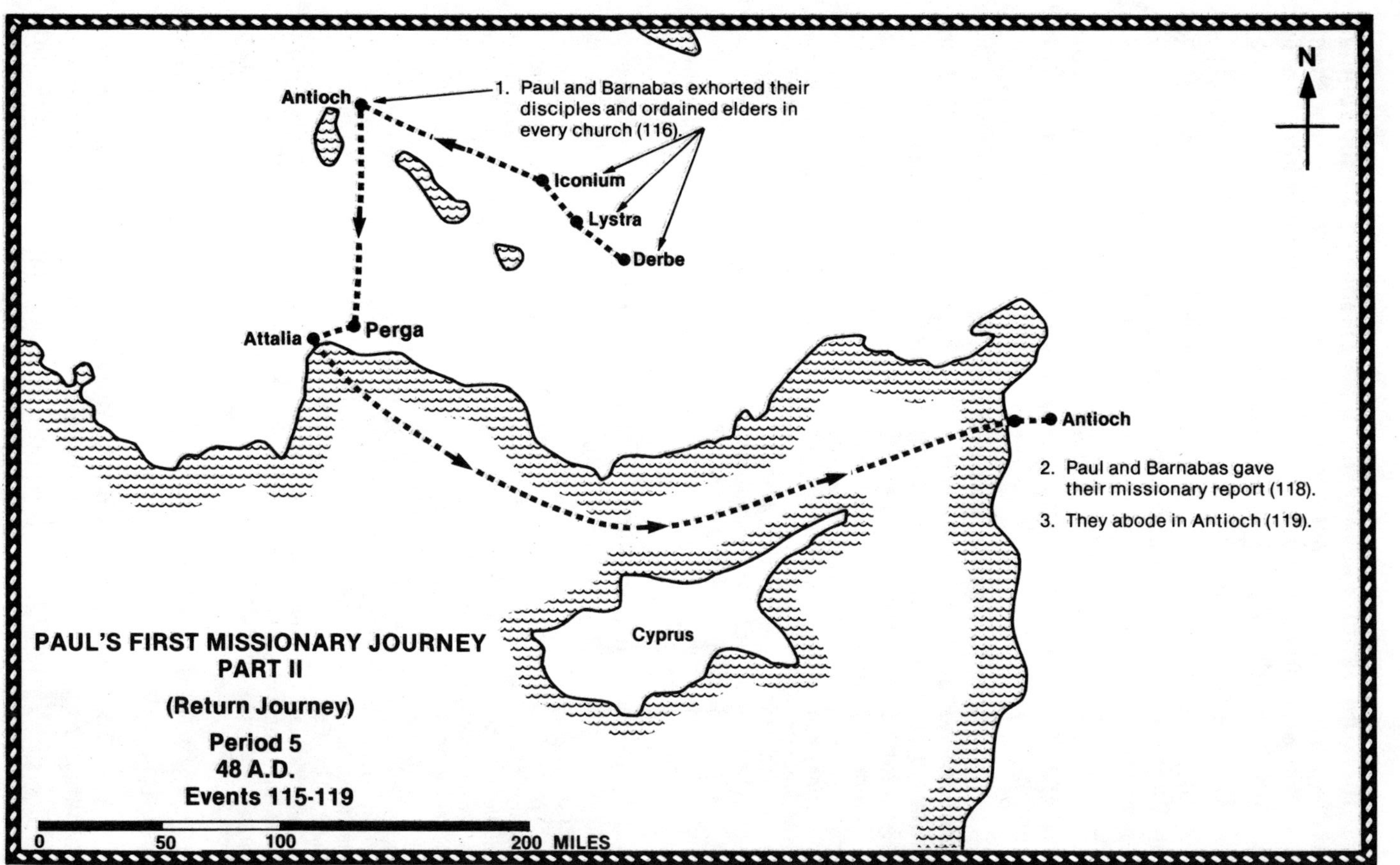
N
Antioch
1. Paul and Barnabas exhorted their disciples and ordained elders in every church (116).
Iconium
Lystra
Derbe
Attalia
Perga
Antioch
2. Paul and Barnabas gave their missionary report (118).
3. They abode in Antioch (119).
Cyprus
PAUL'S FIRST MISSIONARY JOURNEY
PART II
(Return Journey)
Period 5
48 A.D.
Events 115-119
0
50
100
200 MILES

***Note:* Jupiter and Mercury**—Jupiter was the chief god in Roman mythology, the husband of Juno. The Greek equivalent was Zeus. Mercury, in Roman mythology, was the god who served as herald and messenger of the other gods and presided over commerce, eloquence, cunning and theft. The Greek equivalent was Hermes. Barnabas, large in stature, fit the part of the chief god. The eloquent Paul, smaller in stature (2 Cor. 10:10) easily fit the role of spokesman in the eyes of the superstitious populace.

114. Influenced by Jews from Antioch and Iconium, the people of Lystra stoned Paul, carried him out of the city, and left him for dead (14:19). *Lystra; 48 A.D.*

115. Paul, revived and joined by his disciples, returned to Lystra. He then departed with Barnabas to Derbe, where they preached the gospel and taught many (14:20-21). *Lystra to Derbe; 48 A.D.*

116. Paul and Barnabas returned to Lystra, Iconium and Antioch, where they exhorted their disciples and ordained elders in every church (14:21-23). *Derbe to Lystra, Iconium and Antioch; 48 A.D.* ★

117. Paul and Barnabas passed throughout Pisidia, then came to Perga and preached there. They then went to Attalia, and sailed from there back to Antioch to finish their mission (14:24-26). *Pisidia to Perga to Attalia to (Syrian) Antioch; 48 A.D.*

118. In Antioch they gathered the church together and told them all that God had done with them (14:27). *Antioch; 48 A.D.* ★

119. They abode in Antioch a long time with the disciples (14:28). *Antioch; 48-49 A.D.*

APPROXIMATE DISTANCES TRAVELED BY PAUL DURING HIS FIRST MISSIONARY JOURNEY

From	*To*	*Miles Traveled*
Syrian Antioch	Seleucia	15
Seleucia	Salamis	100
Salamis	Paphos	100
Paphos	Perga	175
Perga	Pisidian Antioch	100
Pisidian Antioch	Iconium	85
Iconium	Lystra	30
Lystra	Derbe	30
Derbe	Lystra	30
Lystra	Iconium	30
Iconium	Pisidian Antioch	85
Pisidian Antioch	Perga	100
Perga	Attalia	20
Attalia	Seleucia	320
Seleucia	Syrian Antioch	15
		1,235

Period 6

THE COUNCIL AT JERUSALEM

49 A.D.

Galatians 2:1 to 2:21
Acts 15:1 to 15:35

Peter's Visit to Antioch
Paul Writes His Epistle to the Galatians
Men from Jerusalem Cause a Dispute Concerning Circumcision
Paul, Barnabas and Titus Are Sent to Jerusalem
The Council at Jerusalem
Paul, Barnabas, Judas and Silas Return to Antioch

120. Peter came to Antioch. He ate with the Gentile members, but when other Jewish members came, he and Barnabas and the Jews separated themselves from the Gentiles (according to Jewish law). Paul rebuked them for confusing Jewish laws with the gospel, and for their expecting the Gentile members to live the Jewish laws (Gal. 2:11-21). *Jerusalem to Antioch; 49 A.D.* ★

Note: **The Time of Peter's Visit**—There are various opinions held by different scholars as to when this visit took place. Some say that it occurred after Paul's second visit to Jerusalem to take the famine contributions from the Antioch saints (Acts 11:29-30), placing it between Acts 12:25 and 13:1. Others see it as being connected with the visit of the men from Judea to Antioch (Acts 15:1-6). Still others believe it occurred following the council in Jerusalem, just prior to Paul's second missionary journey (during Acts 15:35). The middle view, which also assumes that the confrontation with Peter was partly the cause for the writing of the Epistle to the Galatians, and that that Epistle was written before the council in Jerusalem, is followed here. There is no certainty on the matter with any of the theories advanced.

121. Paul wrote his Epistle to the Galatians. *Antioch; 49 A.D.*

Note: **The Time of the Writing of Galatians**—The time of the writing of this epistle, and the identity of the churches to which it was addressed, has long been a matter of scholarly debate. The problem centers around this question: Was the epistle written to the churches in southern Galatia which Paul organized on his first missionary journey, or was it written to a group of churches in Galatia proper, which were founded on Paul's second and third missionary journeys? Both lines of thinking are linked to questions concerning the council at Jerusalem. Those who accept the "south Galatian" theory generally hold that the epistle was written from Antioch, just prior to the Jerusalem council. Those who accept the "northern Galatia" theory believe it was written from Macedonia or Ephesus during his third journey.

122. Men from Judea came to Antioch and taught that "Except ye be circumcised after the manner of Moses, ye cannot be saved." **Paul and Barnabas had a major disputation with them (15:1-2).** *Jerusalem to Antioch; 49 A.D.*

Note: **The Debate Over Accountability to Jewish Law**—A major problem which faced the early church was understanding if it was a Jewish Church or if it was a church open to people of all nationalities. They struggled with the doctrinal question of whether they were still expected to live the Law of Moses, and that question embraced questions such as circumcision, dietary laws, restrictions concerning associating with people of other nationalities, how to treat foods used in the worship of other gods, etc. Those who believed that obedience to the Law of Moses was still required of the members of the church were called "Judaizers." Many of them were Pharisees who had been converted to Christianity but still clung to their former beliefs. In chapter 15 of Acts, the matter comes to a head and a decision is reached—though the early members found it difficult to abide by that decision.

123. Paul and Barnabas (and Titus?) and others were sent to the apostles and elders in Jerusalem about the question. They passed through Phoenicia and Samaria, causing great joy to the brethren as they declared the conversion of the Gentiles (15:3). *Antioch to Jerusalem; 49 A.D.*

Note: **Titus**—He was a Greek convert (Gal. 2:3), converted by Paul (Titus 1:4). He probably accompanied Paul to Jerusalem, and it appears that the question of whether or not he needed to be circumcised became a test case. Though that circumcision was not required (Acts 15:28), it appears that he may have been circumcised anyway (Gal. 2:3). He worked closely with Paul in Paul's later ministries, and is mentioned nine times in 2 Corinthians. The question of whether Titus accompanied Paul to Jerusalem in this instance is based on the interpretation of Gal. 2:1-10.

124. They were received of the church and of the apostles and elders at Jerusalem. When they declared what God had done (in their work with the Gentiles), certain of the believers who were Pharisees said that: "It was needful to circumcise them, and to command them to keep the law of Moses" **(15:4-5).** *Jerusalem; 49 A.D.*

125. The apostles and elders held a council to consider the question (15:6). *Jerusalem; 49 A.D.*

126. After much disputing, Peter said: "God put no difference between us and them, purifying their hearts by faith. Now why . . . put a yoke upon the neck of the disciples, which neither our fathers nor we were able to bear?" **(15:7-11).** *Jerusalem, at the council; 49 A.D.* ★

127. The multitude listened while Barnabas and Paul declared what miracles and wonders God had worked among the Gentiles by them (15:12). *Jerusalem, at the council; 49 A.D.* ★

128. James' response (and the decision of the conference): *"My sentence is, that we trouble not . . . the Gentiles [with circumcision, and with responsibility to keep the law of Moses] but we write them to abstain from pollutions of idols, fornication, things*

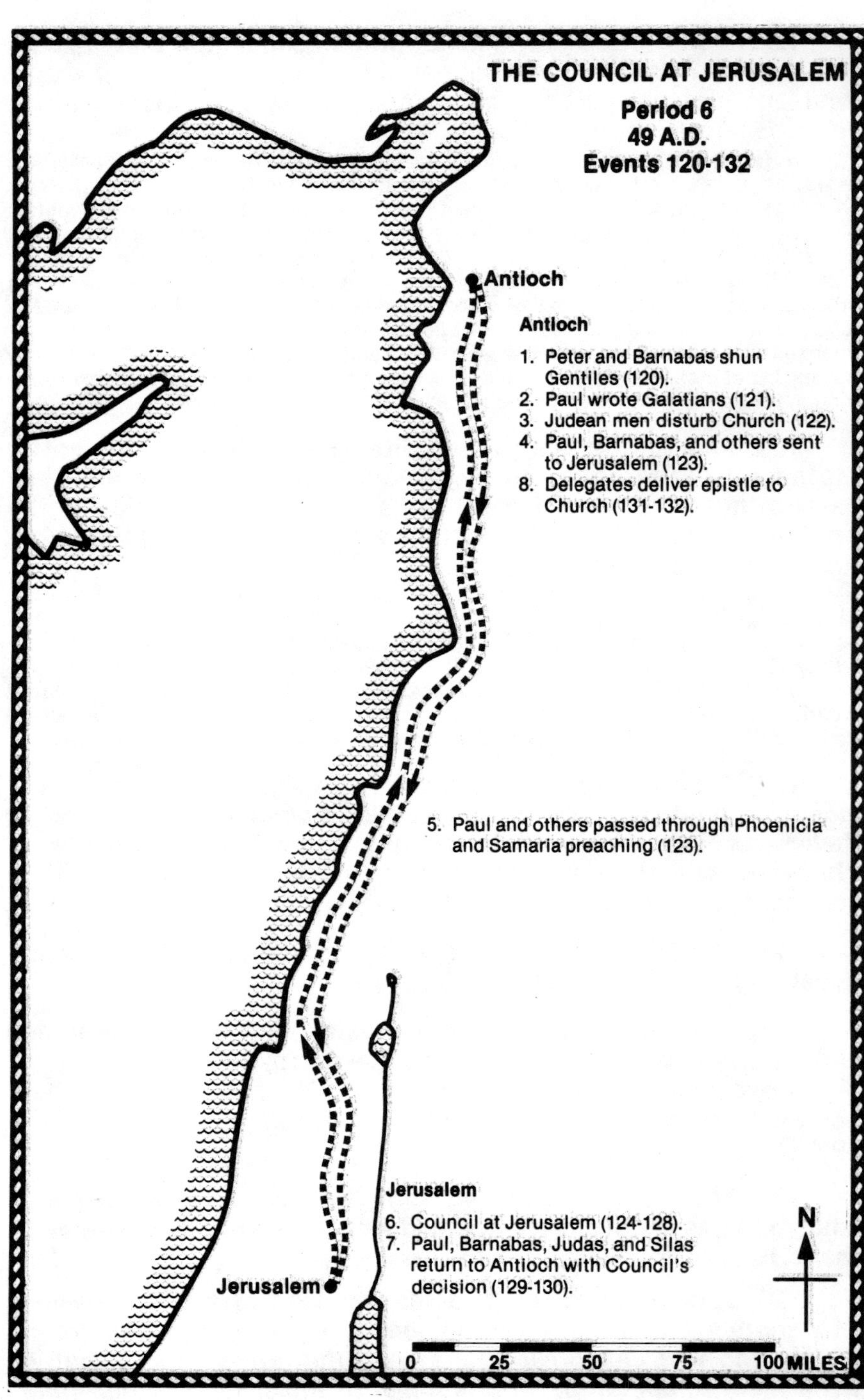
THE COUNCIL AT JERUSALEM
Period 6
49 A.D.
Events 120-132
Antioch
Antioch
1. Peter and Barnabas shun Gentiles (120).
2. Paul wrote Galatians (121).
3. Judean men disturb Church (122).
4. Paul, Barnabas, and others sent to Jerusalem (123).
8. Delegates deliver epistle to Church (131-132).
5. Paul and others passed through Phoenicia and Samaria preaching (123).
Jerusalem
6. Council at Jerusalem (124-128).
7. Paul, Barnabas, Judas, and Silas return to Antioch with Council's decision (129-130).
Jerusalem
N
0
25
50
75
100 MILES

strangled, and from blood **(15:13-21).** *Jerusalem, at the council; 49 A.D.* ★

Note: James—This was James, the brother of the Lord Jesus Christ, who was over the local church in Jerusalem. Tradition holds that he was surnamed "the Just," that he was a Nazarite who abstained from strong drink and animal food, and that he was slain by the scribes and Pharisees, who cast him down from the pinnacle of the temple, then stoned him and clubed him to death. It is interesting that a local official presided in this council which was called to decide a matter of church-wide importance, and that his view was that ultimately accepted by the members in attendance.

129. The apostles, elders, and the church sent Paul and Barnabas to carry letters telling the decision of the council back to the church members at Antioch. They were accompanied by Judas (Barsabas) and Silas, chief men among the brethren (15:22). *Jerusalem to Antioch; 49 A.D.*

Note: Judas and Silas—*Judas*, who was surnamed Barsabas (Barsabbas), may have been a brother to the Joseph Barsabas who was considered as a candidate for the apostleship when Matthias was chosen (Acts 1:23-26). He was probably of Israelite lineage. *Silas* was probably a Helenist, as is indicated by his Latin name (Silas = Silvanus). He was a Roman citizen (Acts 16:37). Little is known about these two men except that they were "chief men among the brethren" (Acts 15:22) and that they were prophets (Acts 15:32). Silas accompanied Paul on his second missionary journey (Acts 16:19; 17:4, 10, 14; 18:5; 2 Cor. 1:19), and was the messenger who delivered Peter's first epistle (1 Pet. 5:12).

130. The letters from the church leaders: "It seemeth good . . . to lay upon you no greater burden than these unnecessary things; that ye abstain from meats offered to idols, blood, strangled things, and from fornication" **(15:23-29).** *Jerusalem to Antioch; 49 A.D.* ★

131. When they came to Antioch, they gathered the multitude and delivered the epistle. Judas and Silas exhorted the brethren. After awhile, Judas returned while Silas stayed in Antioch (15:30-34). *Antioch; 49 A.D.*

132. Paul and Barnabas continued in Antioch (15:35). *Antioch; 49 A.D.*

THE CAESARS OF ROME DURING NEW TESTAMENT TIMES

Name	*Birth*	*Death*	*Reign*
Julius Caesar	102/100 B.C.	44 B.C.	Dictator 49-44 B.C.
Augustus	63 B.C.	A.D. 14	Emperor 27 B.C.-A.D. 14
Tiberius	42 B.C.	A.D. 37	Emperor A.D. 14-37
Gaius Caligula	A.D. 12	A.D. 41	Emperor A.D. 37-41
Claudius	10 B.C.	A.D. 54	Emperor A.D. 41-54
Nero	A.D. 37	A.D. 68	Emperor A.D. 54-68
Galba	3 B.C.	A.D. 69	Emperor A.D. 6/68-1/69
Otho	A.D. 32	A.D. 69	Emperor A.D. 1/15-4/16/69
Vitellius	A.D. 15	A.D. 69	Emperor A.D. 1/2-12/22/69
Vespasian	A.D. 9	A.D. 79	Emperor A.D. 69-79
Titus	A.D. 39/41	A.D. 81	Emperor A.D.79-81
Domitian	A.D. 51	A.D. 96	Emperor A.D. 81-96

Period 7

PAUL'S SECOND MISSIONARY JOURNEY

49 A.D. to 52 A.D.

Acts 15:36 to 18:23

Paul Visits the Churches of Galatia with Silas and Timothy
At Troas Paul Receives a Vision Calling Him into Macedonia
Luke Joined the Missionaries at Troas
Paul Converts Lydia at Philippi
Paul Casts Out an Unclean Spirit at Philippi
Paul and Silas Are Beaten and Imprisoned at Philippi
Freed by an Earthquake, They Baptize the Jailor at Philippi
Paul Preaches to the Jews, then the Gentiles at Thessalonica
Paul and Silas are Sent Away by Night to Berea
Paul Gives His Discourse on Mars Hill at Athens
Paul Sends Timothy and Silas to Confirm the Macedonian Churches
Paul Teaches for Eighteen Months in Corinth
Paul Writes 1 and 2 Thessalonians
Paul Sails to Ephesus with Priscilla and Aquila
Paul Reports to the Church at Jerusalem

133. Paul suggested to Barnabas that they revisit their brethren in every city where they had preached the word (15:36). *Antioch; 49 A.D.*

134. Barnabas wanted to take John (Mark), but Paul disagreed. The contention became so sharp between them that they separated (15:37-39). *Antioch; 49 A.D.*

135. Barnabas took Mark, and sailed to Cyprus (15:39). *Antioch to Cyprus; 49 A.D.*

136. Paul chose Silas as his companion. They went through Syria and Cilicia, confirming the churches (15:40-41). *Antioch westward through Syria and Cilicia towards Galatia; 49 A.D.*

Note: **Cilicia**—This Roman province stretched from the Cilician Gates to the Mediterranean Sea, and from just east of Corycus to Mt. Amanus. In their administration, the Romans combined it with Syria and Phoenicia. Tarsus was the capital of the province.

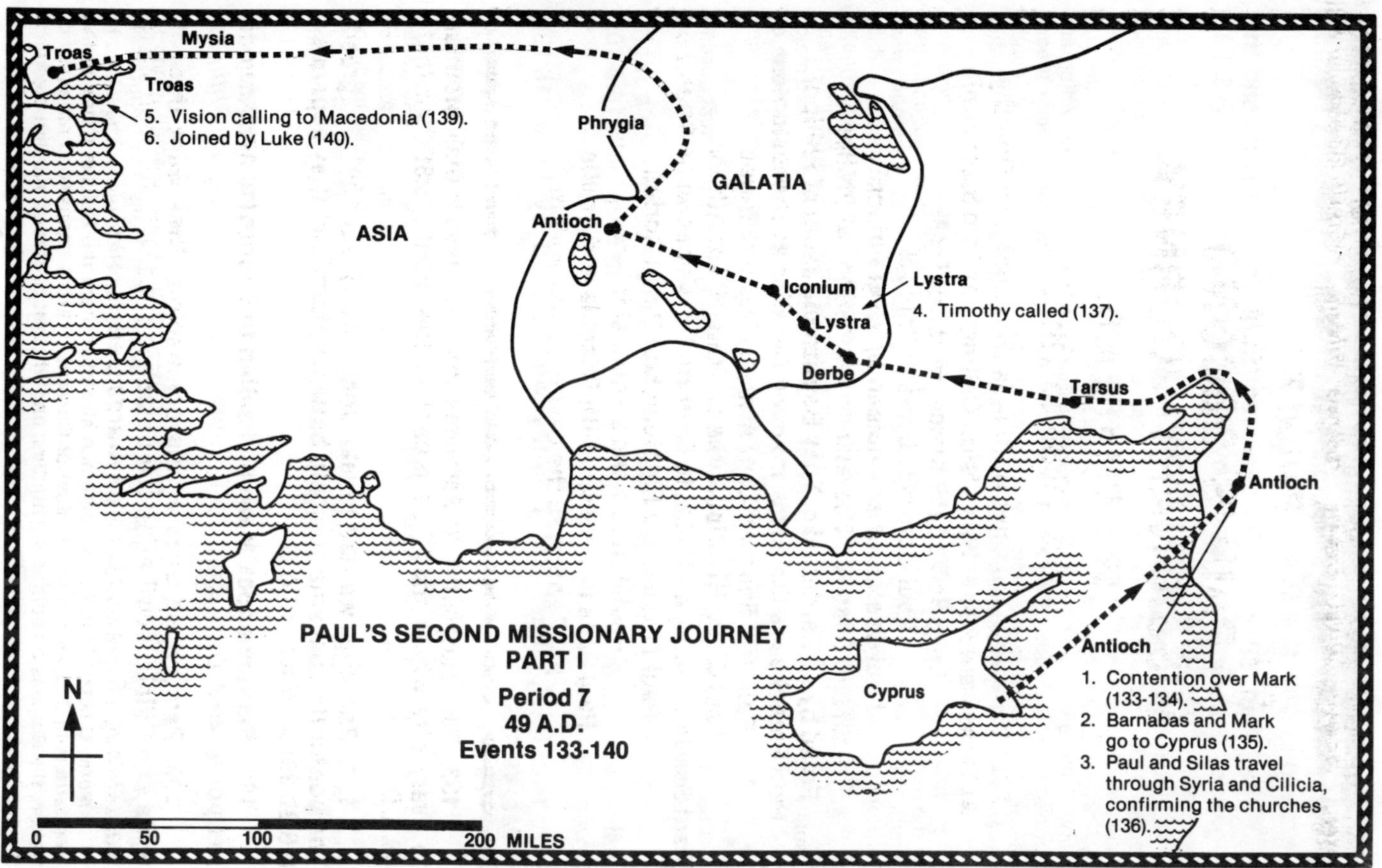
Troas
Mysia
Troas
5. Vision calling to Macedonia (139).
6. Joined by Luke (140).
Phrygia
GALATIA
ASIA
Antioch
Iconium
Lystra
Lystra
4. Timothy called (137).
Derbe
Tarsus
Antioch
Antioch
Cyprus
PAUL'S SECOND MISSIONARY JOURNEY
PART I
Period 7
49 A.D.
Events 133-140
1. Contention over Mark (133-134).
2. Barnabas and Mark go to Cyprus (135).
3. Paul and Silas travel through Syria and Cilicia, confirming the churches (136).
N
0
50
100
200 MILES

137. Paul and Silas came to Derbe, then to Lystra, where Timothy was called to accompany them on their mission (16:1-5). *Derbe to Lystra; 49 A.D.* ★

138. Paul, Silas and Timothy went throughout Phrygia and the region of Galatia. They passed by Mysia and came to Troas (16:6-8). *Lystra to Troas; 49 A.D.* ★

Note: **Phrygia and Galatia**—The *Northern Galatia* theory, previously mentioned, finds its basis in this passage. Those who accept this theory believe that Paul and his party went into the northern area of Galatia, which was once inhabited by Phrygians. They believe that Paul's illness of Gal. 4:13 occurred at this time and allowed the party to linger in the area and found numerous churches which are not named in the book of Acts. Those who adhere to the *Southern Galatia* theory believe that the passage simply indicates that the party visited the churches established on the first missionary journey as they crossed through southern Galatia: Derbe, Lystra, Iconium, and Antioch.

Note: **Asia, Mysia, Bithynia and Troas**—*Asia* was a Roman province, and one of the richest areas in the empire. It was governed by a Roman proconsul and three legati. The most important city was Ephesus. *Mysia* was a district in the northwest territory of Asia, located south of the Hellespont. It was scarcely populated, and its boundaries were not clearly defined. *Bithynia* was a district east of Mysia, though still in the northwest area of Asia minor. In the Roman governing system, it was usually combined with its neighboring district to the east, Pontus. *Troas* was a major city of Asia, located in Mysia on the shores of the Aegean Sea 150 miles north of Ephesus. A seaport city of importance, it was a regular port of call for boats between Macedonia and Asia. The city received many privileges from the Romans, because it was located near the ancient city of Troy, where the Roman people were supposed to have originated.

139. At Troas, a Macedonian man appeared to Paul in a night vision, saying: "Come over into Macedonia, and help us" **(16:9-10).** *Troas; 49 A.D.* ★

140. Paul, Silas, and Timothy were joined by Luke (16:10). *Troas; 49 A.D*

Note: **Luke**—In Acts 16:10 the account suddenly changes from third person to first person, speaking of "we" and "us." Most scholars take this as an indication that Luke, author of the book of Acts, joined the missionary party at Troas. He apparently traveled with them from Troas to Philippi. Luke was a gentile, whom Paul called the "beloved physician" (Col. 4:14). Little is known about him. Some have proposed that he was converted by Paul at Tarsus, and that he may have studied medicine there. In that day physicians often were slaves, though his status is unknown. He is the author of the third gospel as well as the book of Acts. Luke traveled frequently with Paul.

141 The missionaries went to Samothracia, the next day to Neapolis, and from there to Philippi (16:11-12). *Troas to Philippi; 49 A.D.*

Note: **Samothracia, Neapolis, and Philippi**—*Samothracia* is a small island in the northeast Aegean Sea, located about halfway between Troas and Neapolis. It was a regular stop for ships sailing between Syria and the Hellespont. The island is mountainous, and its summit is nearly a mile above sea level. The major city of the island, carrying the same name as the island itself, is on the north side of the island. *Neapolis* was a seaport on the Aegean Sea, on the coast of Macedonia, situated on a mountainous point with a harbor on each side. It served as the port city for Philippi,

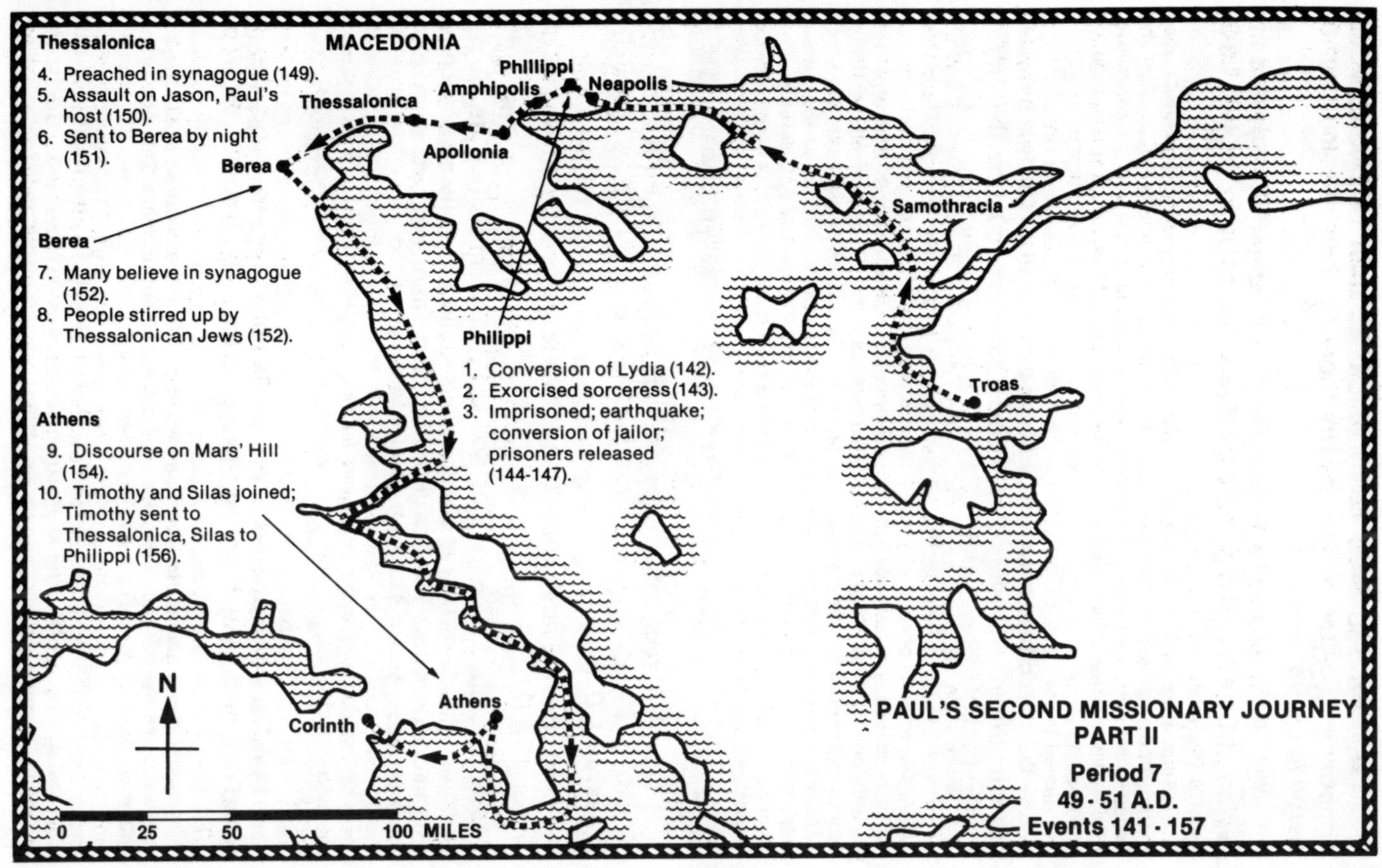

Thessalonica
4. Preached in synagogue (149).
5. Assault on Jason, Paul's host (150).
6. Sent to Berea by night (151).
Berea
7. Many believe in synagogue (152).
8. People stirred up by Thessalonican Jews (152).
Athens
9. Discourse on Mars' Hill (154).
10. Timothy and Silas joined; Timothy sent to Thessalonica, Silas to Philippi (156).
MACEDONIA
Phillippi
Amphipolis
Neapolis
Thessalonica
Apollonia
Berea
Samothracia
Philippi
1. Conversion of Lydia (142).
2. Exorcised sorceress (143).
3. Imprisoned; earthquake; conversion of jailor; prisoners released (144-147).
Troas
N
Athens
Corinth
0
25
50
100 MILES
PAUL'S SECOND MISSIONARY JOURNEY
PART II
Period 7
49 - 51 A.D.
Events 141 - 157

which was situated ten miles inland. The Roman Via Egnatia, the great eastern road which passed through Thessalonica and Philippi, ended in Neapolis. It was customary for people traveling to Asia to end their land travel there and to cross by ship to Troas. The modern name of Neapolis is Kavalla. *Philippi* was a major commercial city of the Roman province of Macedonia. It was located east of Mt. Pangaeus, which was an important source of gold for centuries. To protect that supply of wealth, Philippi had been strongly fortified. The city stood on the side of a steep hill, just north of a large marshy lake. Located near the end of the Via Egnatia, it controlled the flow of east-west travel, and was a place of major significance. The great battle in which Anthony defeated Cassius and Marcus Brutus took place there in 42 B.C. Because of the victory, the city was made a Roman colony. The church which Paul founded there during his second missionary journey was the first Christian church in Europe.

142. The conversion of Lydia and her family. On the Sabbath the missionaries preached to women by a river outside the city of Philippi. Lydia heard and believed. When she and her household were baptized, the missionaries went to live in her home (16:13-15). *Philippi; 49 A.D.* ★

Note: **Lydia**—This lady was Paul's first convert in Europe. She was from Thyatira in Asia's district of Lydia, a city famous for its garment dying industry where beautiful purple cloth was prepared. She was a convert to the Jewish faith, and was a woman of some wealth and position, who had servants and children. In areas where there were limited numbers of Jews, they had no synagogue, but worshipped in open-air situations. Paul apparently sought them in their worship setting, and converted them to Christ.

143. An evil spirit testified of their mission. They encountered a girl possessed with a spirit of divination. She followed them many days, crying: "These men are servants of the most high God, which show unto us the way of salvation." **Paul, grieved, commanded the spirit to come out of her, and he came out (16:16-18).** *Philippi; 49 A.D.* ★

144. Paul and Silas were beaten and imprisoned. The girl's masters caught Paul and Silas and brought them before the magistrates of Philippi, charging them with troubling the city and teaching unlawful customs. The magistrates had them beaten, then cast them into prison (16:19-24). *Philippi; 49 A.D.*

145. Paul and Silas were freed by an earthquake. At midnight an earthquake opened the doors of the prison and loosed everyone's bands. The prison keeper, supposing that his prisoners had fled, drew out his sword to kill himself, but stopped when Paul called out, "We are all here" **(16:25-28).** *Philippi; 49 A.D.*

Note: **Roman procedure concerning escaped prisoners**—It was the Roman custom that if a prisonkeeper (known as a gaoler) allowed a prisoner to escape, he had to assume the prisoner's penalty, be it imprisonment or death. This is why the jailor was ready to take his own life.

146. Conversion and baptism of the jailor. At the mercy of his prisoners, the jailor asked Paul and Silas, "What must I do to be saved?" **They said,** "Believe on the Lord Jesus Christ, and thou shalt be saved, and thy house." **They spoke the word of God to him and his family, and they were baptized (16:29-34).** *Philippi; 49 A.D.* ★

147. Paul's rebuke to the magistrates. When the magistrates sent word that Paul and Silas could be released, Paul said, "They have beaten us openly uncondemned, being Romans. . . . let them come themselves and fetch us out." **The magistrates came and released them, and asked that they leave the city. They departed (16:35-40).** *Philippi; 49 A.D.*

Note: **Roman citizenship and rights accompanying that citizenship**—Roman citizenship gave individuals freedom from degrading punishments frequently inflicted on others, such as being placed in bonds, being scourged, or being crucified. Roman citizenship could be acquired by birth, if both parents were Roman citizens; by purchase, by long service in the Roman army; by grants made to individuals for political or military services; or by grants made to cities or districts. Paul and Silas had been denied the freedoms guaranteed under Roman law, and they made sure the magistrates were fully aware that they had broken the law in their regard.

Note: **Luke remains behind**—At this point the first person "we" ceases to be used. It is believed that Luke remained behind in Philippi for several years, until he rejoined Paul at Troas during his third missionary journey (Acts 20:5). Paul, Silas and Timothy continued into Thessalonica.

148. The missionaries passed through Amphipolis and Apollonia, and came to Thessalonica (17:1). *Philippi to Thessalonica; 49 A.D.*

Note: **Amphipolis and Apollonia**—*Amphipolis* was a town 32 miles west of Philippi on the Via Egnatia, the major Roman road. The Romans had raised it to the rank of a free town, and it was the chief town in that district of the province of Macedonia. It was situated on the river Strymon, about three miles from its mouth, where it flowed into the Aegean Sea. *Apollonia* was another town on the Roman road, about halfway between Amphipolis and Thessalonica. Today it is called Pollina.

149. Paul preached in the synagogue at Thessalonica, saying: "This Jesus, whom I preach unto you, is Christ." **Some of the Jews, and many of the Greeks and women, believed (17:1-4).** *Thessalonica; 49-50 A.D.* ★

Note: **Thessalonica**—This city, now known as Salonika, was the capital of the Roman province of Macedonia. Built on the side of a hill, the city was a large and important commercial center, and a major stopping point on the Via Egnatia.

Note: **The length of Paul's stay in Thessalonica**—Paul's two epistles to the saints at Thessalonica seem to indicate that he must have stayed several months in the city, rather than just three weeks as implied by the "three sabbath days" in verse 2. The epistles show that the church members were primarily gentile members (1 Thes. 1:9; 2:14). Many believe that Paul spent three weeks attempting to convert the Jews of the city, then spent three or four months laboring among the gentiles in the city.

150. The assault upon Jason. The unbelieving Jews gathered a mob, and tried to find the missionaries at the house of Jason, where they were lodging. Not finding them, they took Jason and other brethren unto the city rulers, charging that "These all do contrary to the decrees of Caesar, saying that there is another king, one Jesus." **The rulers took security of the brethren, then released them (17:5-9).** *Thessalonica; 49 A.D.* ★

151. Paul and Silas were sent away by night unto Berea (17:10). *Thessalonica to Berea; 50 A.D.*

Note: **Berea**—This Macedonian town was located about 50 miles southwest of Thessalonica. It had a large population in Paul's day. The Greek name of the town today is Verria.

152. Paul and Silas made many converts in the synagogue at Berea, until the Jews from Thessalonica came and stirred up the people against them (17:10-14). *Berea; 50 A.D.* ★

153. Paul went by sea to Athens, and sent word to Silas and Timothy to quickly join him (17:14-15). *Berea to Athens; 50 A.D.*

Note: **Athens**—From the fifth century B.C., when it was the most important of the Greek democracies, Athens still held its preeminence as a city of artistic, literary, cultural and commercial supremacy. Socrates, Plato, and Aristotle all lived and taught there. After Rome conquered the Greeks, it became part of the Roman province of Achaia. In Paul's day, the city was considered the intellectual center of the world. The city is about three miles inland from the seacoast, and lies on a plain. The Acropolis (the citadel on the hill which overlooks the city) and the nearby Parthenon were dedicated to Athena, the Greek goddess of wisdom and women's crafts.

154. Paul's discourse on Mars' Hill to the Epicurean and Stoick philosophers: "We are the offspring of God. . . . He will judge the world . . . by that man whom he hath ordained; . . . he hath raised him from the dead" **(17:16-33).** *Athens; 50 A.D.* ***[★ —Major Discourse #7]***

Note: **Mars' Hill**—This is a rocky hill 380 feet high, located northwest of the Acropolis and connected to it by a ridge. The hill, called Areopagus by the Greeks (meaning "hill of Ares"—the Greek god of war, corresponding to Mars, the Roman god of war), had become the meeting place of the aristocratic council which held political power including the supervision of education and the right to control the introduction of new religious or philosophical teachings.

Note: **The Greek philosophers**—Athens was the world's center of learning in Paul's day. Its university was the most renowned of all places of higher learning, and students came from all over the Roman empire. The city was also where philosophical thought came into being, and it was the home of the major philosophical schools of Paul's day. The city contained famous sites related to former philosophers, including the Academy of Plato, the Garden of Epicurus, the Porch of Zeno, and the Lyceum of Aristotle. In Paul's day, however, only two philosophies were of major importance: Stoicism and Epicureanism.

Stoicism was a philosophical school founded by the Greek Zeno about 278 B.C. It was a system of pantheistic monism. In this philosophy, virtue was regarded as the highest good, ethics were very austere, and the philosophy's adherents were unmoved by pain or pleasure. They rejected compromise, and believed a man should suffer persecution and even death rather than leave the path of virtue and piety. They were fatalists, and denied the freedom of the will. The Stoics believed in a Divine Reason, or Logos, which ordered all things of the world, though they regarded it as the soul of the world rather than as a personal being. They also believed that man had a future life, and they were devoted to the Law of Nature, which they regarded as being an actual code which the Creator had imposed upon man. The philosophy of the Stoics was very similar to the beliefs of the Jewish Pharisees.

In Paul's day, the majority of the serious-minded people embraced the philosophy of the Stoics, while Epicureanism was the philosophy of the irreligious and frivilous people. The *Epicureans* were followers of the Greek Epicurus (341-270 B.C.). He taught that the chief purpose of man is to achieve happiness. In this belief, the greatest joy for the philosopher was to follow mental and intellectual pursuits, but for others lower goals of sensual pleasure provided the greatest satisfaction. Thus the philosophy gained a bad reputation. The Epicureans denied the governing influence of God in human affairs, and did not believe that man's existence continued after death.

The teachings of Christianity, such as a belief in divine creation, judgment, resurrection, etc., were much closer to the views of the Stoics than to the beliefs of the Epicureans.

155. Dionysius, Damaris, and others believed Paul (17:34). *Athens; 50 A.D.*

Note: **Dionysius**—This convert was an Areopagite, or in other words a member of the council of the Areopagus. He must have been a person of high social position. Tradition portrays him as a bishop of Athens and a Christian martyr.

156. Timothy and Silas joined Paul in Athens, then Paul sent them out to confirm the churches. Timothy was sent back to Thessalonica (1 Thes. 3:1-7); Silas apparently was sent to Philippi, leaving Paul alone in Athens. They rejoined Paul in Corinth (18:5). *Athens to Thessalonica and Philippi; 50 A.D.* ★

157. Paul came to Corinth (18:1) *Athens to Corinth; 50 A.D.*

Note: **Corinth**—This city was the capital of the Roman province of Achaia. It stood on the four-mile-wide neck of land which connected mainland Greece with the Peloponnese, a southern peninsula. It had two adjoining ports: Cenchreae, on the Aegean Sea, and Lechaeum on the Gulf of Lepanto. In Paul's day small ships were hauled across the isthmus on a track, which saved several hundred miles of sailing. Corinth was the second most important city of Achaia, surpassed only by Athens. It was a major stopover on the sea routes of the day, with the next stop to the east being Ephesus. The city had a citadel on a hill 1800 feet high, and it was also defended by a high wall which reached all the way to the Lechaeum harbor. The maritime city was always filled with traders and travelers, and most of the traffic between Italy and Asia passed through the city. The people of the city worshipped Venus, the Roman goddess of love and beauty (Greek: Aphrodite), and the ritual fornication involved in this worship had made the city a place of moral degradation.

158. Paul stayed with Aquila and Priscilla, and joined them in their mutual craft: tentmaking (18:2-3). *Corinth; 50 A.D.*

Note: **Aquila and Priscilla**—Aquila was a Jew from Pontus, and made his living as a leather mechant. He and his wife Prisca (Priscilla is a diminutive form of Prisca) lived in Rome until they were driven out of that city by the edict of Claudius in 49 A.D. They probably were already Christians before Paul encountered them, though how they were converted is not known. Paul stayed in their home, and as his second missionary journey drew to an end, they traveled with him to Ephesus, where they were instrumental in converting Apollos (Acts 18:18, 26).

Note: **Claudius Caesar**—Claudius, the fourth Roman Caesar, ruled from 41-54 A.D. He gave the Jews the right to religious freedom, but he banished them from Rome in 49 A.D. (Acts 18:2). The famine prophesied by Agabus (Acts 11:28) took place during his reign. His rule was generally considered a period of unrest and distress across the entire Mediterranean world.

159. Silas and Timothy came from Macedonia and rejoined Paul (18:5). They brought funds supplied by the churches in Macedonia which helped Paul in his missionary work (2 Cor. 11:9). *Corinth; 50 A.D.*

160. Paul rebuked the Jews and turned to the Gentiles. When the Corinthian Jews opposed Paul's message that "Jesus was Christ," he shook his raiment at them, saying, "Your blood be upon your own heads; I am clean: from henceforth I will go unto the Gentiles" **(18:4-6).** *Corinth; 50 A.D.* ★

161. Paul stayed at the home of Justus. Crispus, chief ruler in the synagogue, believed on the Lord. Many of the Corinthians, when they heard of his conversion, believed and were baptized (18:7-8). *Corinth; 50 A.D.* ★

162. The Lord spoke to Paul in a vision: "Be not afraid, but speak, . . . I am with thee, and no man shall set on thee to hurt thee: for I have much people in this city" **(18:9-10).** *Corinth; 50 A.D.* ★

163. Paul remained at Corinth eighteen months, teaching the word of God among them (18:11). *Corinth; 50-51 A.D.*

Note: **Paul's converts at Corinth**—Many of Paul's converts in Corinth are named in the New Testament. They include Crispus (Acts 18:8), Stephanas (1 Cor. 16:15), Fortunatus (1 Cor. 16:17), Achaicus (1 Cor. 16:17), Erastus (Rom. 16:23), Gaius (1 Cor. 1:14), Tertius (Rom. 16:22), Quartus (Rom. 16:23), Sosthenes (1 Cor. 1:1), Chloe (1 Cor. 1:11), and Phoebe of Cenchrea (Rom. 16:1).

164. Paul wrote his first epistle to the Thessalonians. *Corinth; 51 A.D.*

Note: **First Thessalonians**—This epistle was apparently occasioned by Timothy's report of problems which he encountered when he returned to strengthen the church at Thessalonica (see #157, 160). It was written from Corinth about 51 A.D.

165. Paul wrote his second epistle to the Thessalonians. *Corinth; 51 A.D.*

Note: **Second Thessalonians**—This epistle was also written from Corinth, not more than a few months after his first letter was sent. These two epistles, together with the epistle to the Galatians and the epistle of James, are the earliest-written books of the New Testament.

Note: **Four Groups of Pauline Epistles**—The epistles of Paul are often classified as falling into four groups, separated from the other epistles by lengthy periods of time. The two epistles written to the Thessalonians are considered his first group of letters—those written during his second missionary journey. (Galatians, if it was written prior to the second missionary journey, is also classified in this group.) The second group was written during his third missionary journey and includes 1st and 2nd Corinthians, Galatians (if the earlier time of writing is not accepted), and Romans. The third group, which includes Philippians, Colossians, Ephesians, and Philemon, was written during his first captivity in Rome. The final group, written near the end of his life, includes 1st and 2nd Timothy, and Titus.

166. The Jews brought Paul to the judgment seat, when Gallio was the deputy of Achaia, saying, "This fellow persuadeth men to worship God contrary to the law." **Gallio replied,** "If it be a question of words and names, and of your law, look ye to it; for I will be no judge of such matters." **He sent them away (18:12-16).** *Corinth; 51 A.D.*

Note: **Gallio**—This ruler was the older brother of Seneca, Nero's tutor, and the uncle of the poet Lucan. He was proconsul of Achaia in 51-52 A.D. An inscription at Delphi indicates that he began his service there on July 1, A.D. 51.

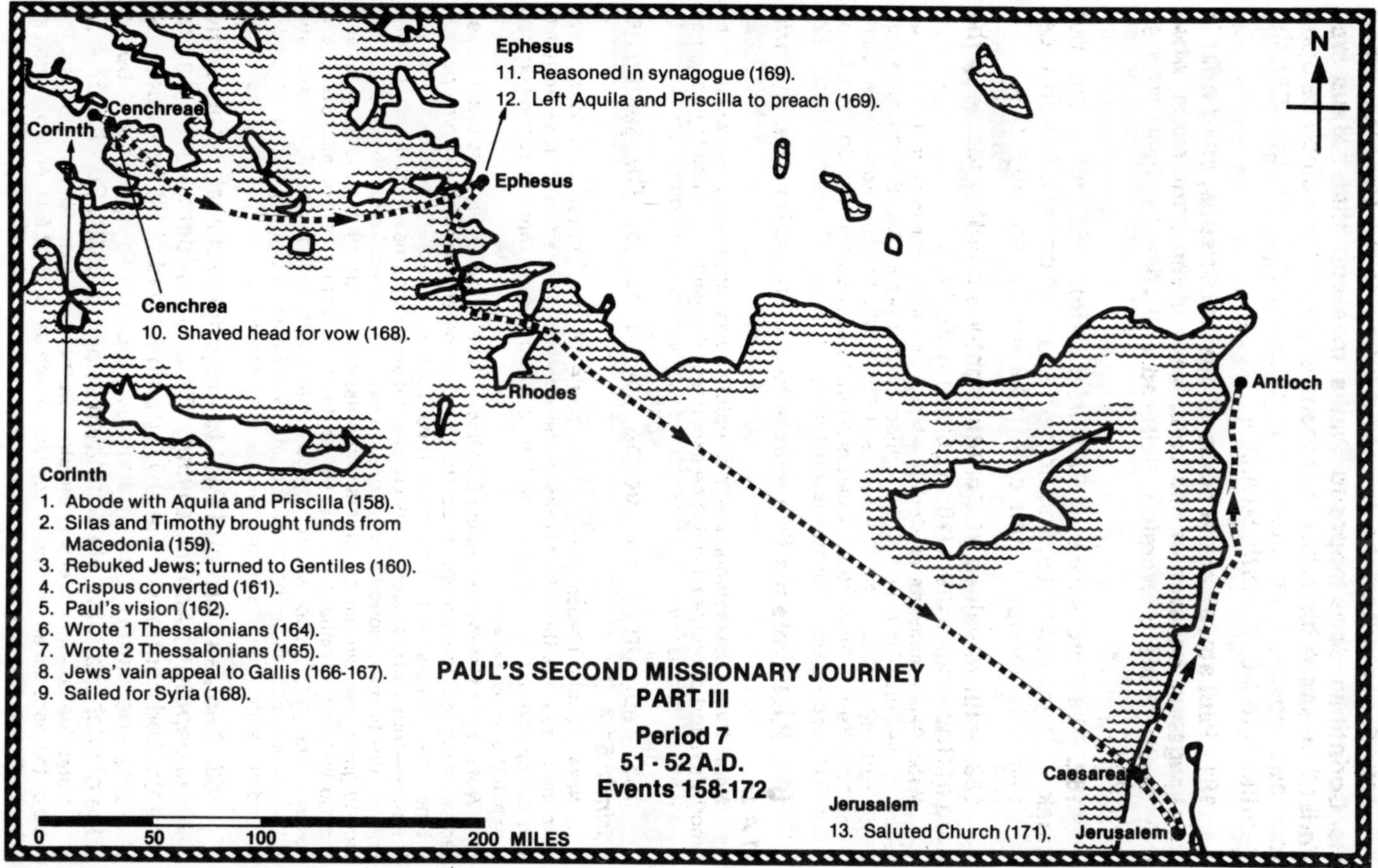
Ephesus
11. Reasoned in synagogue (169).
12. Left Aquila and Priscilla to preach (169).
N
Cenchreae
Corinth
Ephesus
Cenchrea
10. Shaved head for vow (168).
Rhodes
Antioch
Corinth
1. Abode with Aquila and Priscilla (158).
2. Silas and Timothy brought funds from Macedonia (159).
3. Rebuked Jews; turned to Gentiles (160).
4. Crispus converted (161).
5. Paul's vision (162).
6. Wrote 1 Thessalonians (164).
7. Wrote 2 Thessalonians (165).
8. Jews' vain appeal to Gallis (166-167).
9. Sailed for Syria (168).
PAUL'S SECOND MISSIONARY JOURNEY
PART III
Period 7
51 - 52 A.D.
Events 158-172
Caesarea
Jerusalem
13. Saluted Church (171).
Jerusalem
0
50
100
200 MILES

167. The Greeks took the chief ruler of the synagogue, Sosthenes, and beat him before the judgment seat. Gallio did not consider the matter (18:17). *Corinth; 51 A.D.*

168. Paul sailed homeward (to Syria), traveling with Priscilla and Aquila. He shaved his head in Cenchrea, for he had a vow (18:18). *Corinth to Cenchrea, sailing to Ephesus; early fall, 51 A.D.*

Note: **Shaving the Head as a Sign of a Vow**—Many Jews were accustomed to follow a modified form of the Nazarite vow (Num. 6). This was often done after recovering from sickness or after being delivered from danger. The custom was to present the hair grown during the time of the vow at the altar at Jerusalem, along with the performance of special sacrifices. This meant that the head was shaved at the beginning of the vow, and at the end of the vow period. This was probably Paul's way of thanking God for his safety during his missionary journey.

169. When they arrived at Ephesus, Paul left Priscilla and Aquila there. He reasoned with the Jews in the synagogue, then bid them farewell saying, "I must by all means keep this feast that cometh in Jerusalem" **(18:19-21).** *Ephesus; fall 51 A.D.*

Note: **The Feast at Jerusalem**—This feast was probably either the Passover or Pentecost, held in the spring of 52 A.D.

170. Paul sailed from Ephesus and landed at Caesarea (18:21-22). *Ephesus to Caesarea; winter, 52 A.D.*

171. Paul went up to Jerusalem and saluted the church (18:22). *Caesarea to Jerusalem; spring, 52 A.D.*

172. Paul returned to Antioch and spent some time there (18:22-23). *Jerusalem to Antioch; spring and summer, 52 A.D.*

APPROXIMATE DISTANCES TRAVELED BY PAUL DURING HIS SECOND MISSIONARY JOURNEY

From	*To*	*Miles Traveled*
Syrian Antioch	Cilician Gates	140
Cilician Gates	Derbe	100
Derbe	Lystra	30
Lystra	Iconium	30
Iconium	Pisidian Antioch	85
Pisidian Antioch	Phrygia and Galatia	200+
Phrygia and Galatia	Troas	200+
Troas	Samothrace	70
Samothrace	Neapolis	70
Neapolis	Philippi	10
Philippi	Amphipolis	30
Amphipolis	Apollonia	35
Apollonia	Thessalonica	40
Thessalonica	Berea	50
Berea	the coast	20
the coast	Athens	250
Athens	Corinth	50
Corinth	Cenchrea	8
Cenchrea	Ephesus	250
Ephesus	Caesarea	650+
Caesarea	Jerusalem	65
Jerusalem	Syrian Antioch	320+
		2,703+

Period 8

PAUL'S THIRD MISSIONARY JOURNEY

52 A.D. to 57 A.D.

Acts 18:23 to 21:15

Paul Visits the Disciples in Galatia and Phrygia
Paul Labors in Ephesus for "Three Years"
Ephesian Converts Baptized with John's Baptism are Rebaptized
Paul's Unrecorded Visit and Letter to Corinth
Vagabond Sons of Sceva are Overcome by an Evil Spirit
Paul writes 1 and 2 Corinthians, Galatians?, and Romans
(the second group of Pauline epistles)
Demetrius Agitates the Ephesian Silversmiths Against Paul
Paul Travels through Macedonia
Paul Labors for Three Months in Corinth
Paul Restores Eutychus to Life at Troas
Paul's Farewell to the Ephesian Church at Miletus

173. Paul left Antioch and went over all Galatia and Phrygia, strengthening the disciples (18:23). *Antioch through Galatia and Phrygia; fall, 52 A.D.*

Note: **The Churches in Galatia and Phrygia**—If Paul visited all the disciples, his journey probably included brief visits to the converts in Derbe, Lystra, and Iconium in Galatia, and to Antioch in Phrygia (sometimes referred to as "Pisidian Antioch"). Those who accept the *Northern Galatia* theory believe that this visit also included a visit to other unnamed churches farther north in Galatia.

174. Paul instructed the churches of Galatia to participate in the collection for the saints in Jerusalem (1 Cor. 16:1-2). *Galatia; fall, 52 A.D.*

175. The visit of Apollos to Ephesus. Apollos came to Ephesus and taught diligently the things of the Lord. Since he knew only the baptism of John (the Baptist), Aquila and Priscilla "expounded unto him the way of God more perfectly" **(18:24-26).** *Ephesus; 53 A.D.* ★

Note: **Apollos**—Apollos was a highly educated Jew from Alexandria. His name is an abbreviated form of Apollonios, or Apollodoros or Apollonides. After preaching in Ephesus he went on to Corinth, where he preached with such power and charisma that an Apollos party formed within the Church. Paul wrote to the Corinthian saints

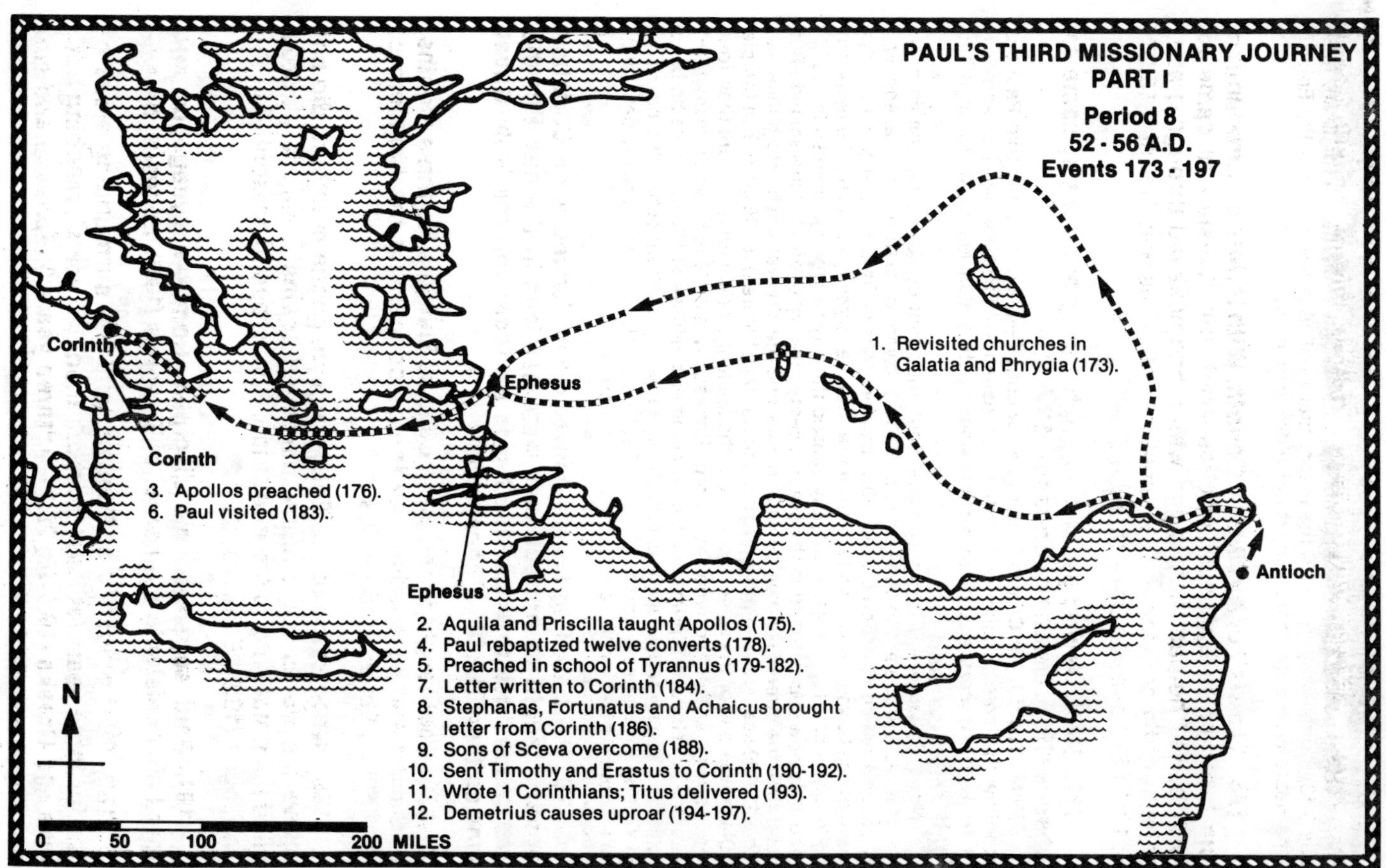
PAUL'S THIRD MISSIONARY JOURNEY
PART I
Period 8
52 - 56 A.D.
Events 173 - 197
1. Revisited churches in Galatia and Phrygia (173).
Corinth
Ephesus
Corinth
3. Apollos preached (176).
6. Paul visited (183).
Antioch
Ephesus
2. Aquila and Priscilla taught Apollos (175).
4. Paul rebaptized twelve converts (178).
5. Preached in school of Tyrannus (179-182).
7. Letter written to Corinth (184).
8. Stephanas, Fortunatus and Achaicus brought letter from Corinth (186).
9. Sons of Sceva overcome (188).
10. Sent Timothy and Erastus to Corinth (190-192).
11. Wrote 1 Corinthians; Titus delivered (193).
12. Demetrius causes uproar (194-197).
N
0
50
100
200 MILES

that "I have planted, Apollos watered; but God gave the increase." (1 Cor. 3:6). It appears that Apollos later carried Paul's epistle to Titus on the isle of Crete (see Titus 3:13). Some have proposed the theory that Apollos is the author of the Epistle to the Hebrews, though that theory is not widely accepted.

176. *The visit of Apollos to Corinth.* With letters of introduction from brethren in Ephesus, Apollos went into Achaia and came to Corinth. He "helped them much which had believed through grace: for he mightly convinced the Jews . . . that Jesus was Christ" **(18:27-28; 19:1).** *Ephesus to Corinth; 53 A.D.* ★

177. Paul, having passed through the upper coasts, came to Ephesus (19:1). *Galatia to Ephesus; 53 A.D.*

***Note:* The "Upper Coasts" or "Upper Country"**—Luke indicates that Paul did not follow the more popular level route to Ephesus through Colossae and Laodicea, but traveled the northern, more mountainous route which led down through the Cayster valley.

***Note:* Ephesus**—This city was the most important center in the Roman province of Asia. It stood at the western end of the caravan route through Asia, and was the seaport which connected Asia with the countries to the west. It stood at the mouth of the Cayster River, and silt from the river was already clogging the harbor in Paul's day, a problem which eventually caused the city to greatly diminish in importance. (It is now separated from the sea by twenty miles of reed-filled marshland.) But at that time the streets were paved with marble, and the city was one of magnificence, with a 25,000-seat arena, libraries, and a population of more than 350,000. The temple of Diana was one of the seven wonders of the ancient world, and was more than four times as large as the Parthenon at Athens. Ephesus was a place to which many tourists came on religious pilgrimages, and as commerce declined because of the harbor's problems, the city turned more and more to trades related to meeting the needs of the visiting worshippers and tourists. In Paul's day, the city was already declining, and able only to bask in its reputation of former greatness.

178. Paul, finding twelve converts who lacked valid Christian baptism, taught them and "they were baptized in the name of the Lord Jesus." **He then laid his hands on them and the Holy Ghost came on them (19:1-7).** *Ephesus; 53 A.D.* ★

179. Paul taught in the synagogue at Ephesus for three months, "disputing and persuading the things concerning the kingdom of God" **(19:8).** *Ephesus; 54 A.D.* ★

180. When some of the Ephesian synagogue members did not believe his words and became hardened against Paul, they spoke evil of his preaching to the multitude. Paul stopped preaching in the synagogue (19:9). *Ephesus; 54 A.D.*

181. Paul separated his disciples from the synagogue and moved his ministry to the school of Tyrannus (19:9). *Ephesus; 54 A.D.*

182. Paul preached in Ephesus and the surrounding areas of Asia for three years (at least for more than two years), reaching both Jews and Greeks (19:9-10; 20:31 = "three years"). *Ephesus and surrounding areas; 54-56 A.D.*

183. Paul made a visit to Corinth during his ministry in Ephesus (2 Cor. 12:14; 13:1). *Ephesus to Corinth, back to Ephesus; 55 A.D.*

***Note:* Paul's Unrecorded Visit to Corinth**—Little is known about this visit to Corinth, except that it apparently dealt with the correction of some problem of conduct or morality (see 2 Cor. 2:1; 13:2). This visit is not mentioned in Luke's account in Acts, but is alluded to by Paul in his epistles to the Corinthian Church. He wrote that he was ready to visit them a "third time" (2 Cor. 12:14; 13:1), yet Acts has recorded only his visit during his second missionary journey (Acts 18:1-18). Paul referred to this unrecorded visit as characterized by "heaviness" (2 Cor. 2:1) and strife (2 Cor. 12:20-21). Some commentators suggest that Paul's illness of 2 Cor. 12:7-10 occurred while he was in Corinth, and that it was interpreted by his enemies as an indication of divine disfavor and used against Paul to discredit his authority.

***Note:* Visits of Other Leaders and Members to Corinth**—It appears others had visited Corinth, which had caused divisions among the saints. These included Peter (Cephas) (see 1 Cor. 1:12; 3:22), Apollos (see Acts 18:27-28, 19:1; 1 Cor. 1:12; 3:22), and some Jewish Christians who had brought letters of commendation with them from Jerusalem (see 2 Cor. 3:1). Corinth; 53-55 A.D.

184. Paul wrote a letter to the members in Corinth, instructing them "not to company with fornicators" **(1 Cor. 5:9).** *Ephesus; 55 A.D.*

***Note:* Paul's Unpreserved Letter to the Corinthians**—The time and place of the writing of this letter is unknown, except that it obviously was written during the interval after Paul left Corinth, near the end of his second missionary journey and before he wrote his epistle now known as 1 Corinthians from Ephesus during his third missionary journey. It is generally assumed to have been written from Ephesus during the early portion of his two-to-three year stay there, while on his third mission, and shortly after his unrecorded visit to Corinth. Some scholars believe a fragment of this letter is preserved in 2 Cor. 6:14-7:1 or in 2 Cor. 10-13. This letter is termed the "severe letter," as contrasted with the "thankful letter," 2 Cor. 1-9. The latter they believe to be the letter written from Macedonia known today as 2 Corinthians. Ephesus; 55 A.D.

185. Paul received a letter from the Church in Corinth (1 Cor. 7:1). (Paul probably was replying to, or alluding to, this letter in 1 Cor. 5:10; 8:1-10; 10:25; 11:2.) *Ephesus; 55 A.D.*

186. Stephanas, Fortunatus and Achaicus arrived from Corinth with news of the Church there, and probably brought Paul the letter from the Church members at Corinth (1 Cor. 16:17). *Corinth to Ephesus; 55 A.D.*

187 God wrought miracles by the hands of Paul (19:11-12). *Ephesus; 54-56 A.D.* ★

188. The seven vagabond sons of Sceva, without authority, attempted to cast out an evil spirit in the name of Jesus. The evil spirit answered, "Jesus I know, and Paul I know; but who are ye?" **The possessed man leaped on the seven and overcame them. They fled naked and wounded (19:13-16).** *Ephesus; 54-56 A.D.* ★

189. Fear fell on the Jews and Greeks at Ephesus. Many believers confessed their evil deeds. The users of curious arts burned their books (of magic) publicly. The word of God grew and prevailed (19:17-20). *Ephesus; 54-56 A.D.* ★

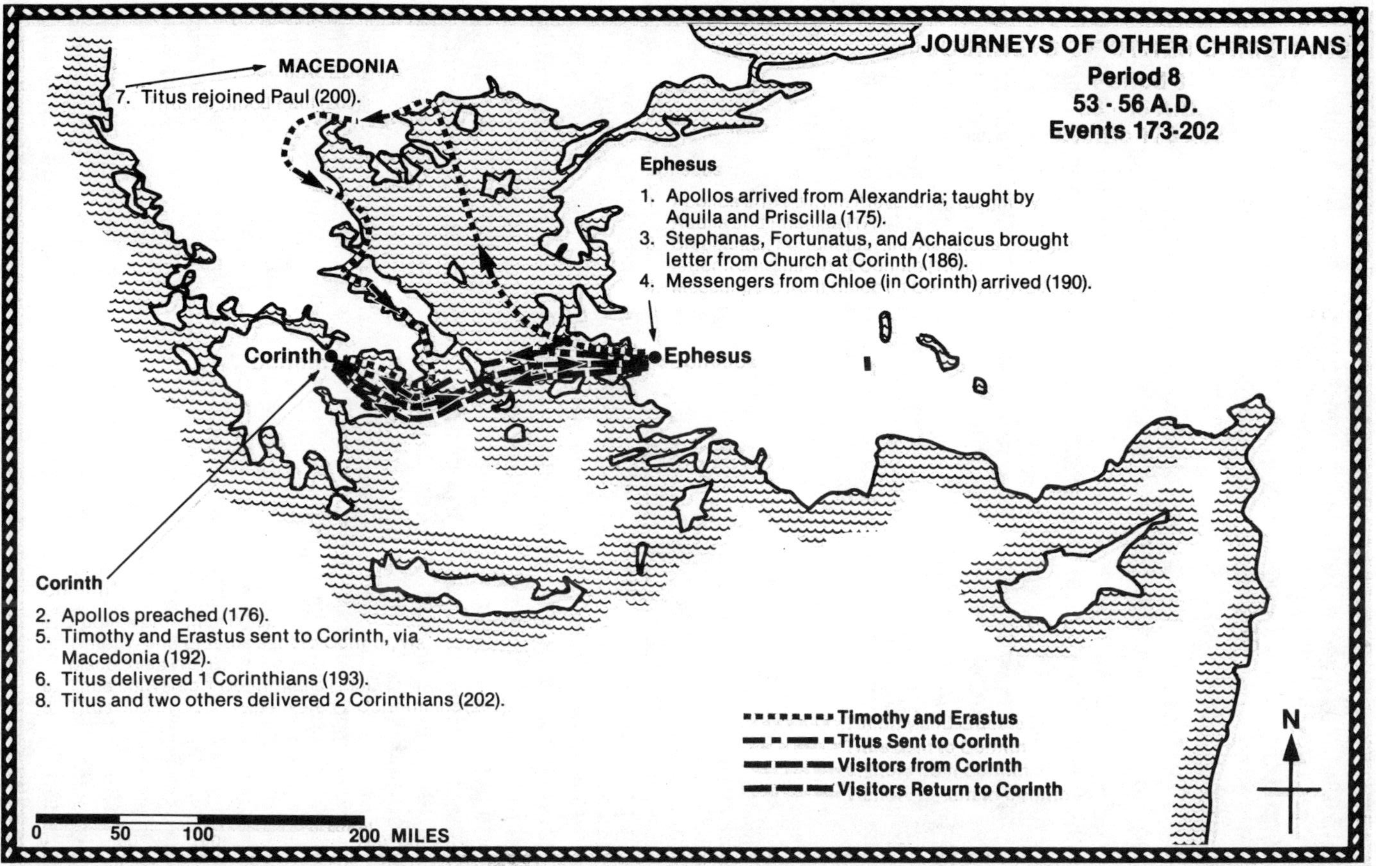
JOURNEYS OF OTHER CHRISTIANS
Period 8
53 - 56 A.D.
Events 173-202
MACEDONIA
7. Titus rejoined Paul (200).
Ephesus
1. Apollos arrived from Alexandria; taught by Aquila and Priscilla (175).
3. Stephanas, Fortunatus, and Achaicus brought letter from Church at Corinth (186).
4. Messengers from Chloe (in Corinth) arrived (190).
Corinth
Ephesus
Corinth
2. Apollos preached (176).
5. Timothy and Erastus sent to Corinth, via Macedonia (192).
6. Titus delivered 1 Corinthians (193).
8. Titus and two others delivered 2 Corinthians (202).
Timothy and Erastus
Titus Sent to Corinth
Visitors from Corinth
Visitors Return to Corinth
N
0
50
100
200 MILES

190. Messengers from Chloe, in Corinth, arrived and informed Paul that there were serious contentions among the saints there (1 Cor. 1:11). Individuals had come to Corinth, with letters of recommendation from other churches, who had spoken against Paul and undermined his teachings and authority (2 Cor. 3:1; 11:5; 2:5-11). *Corinth to Ephesus; 55 A.D.*

191. Paul, in the Spirit, decided to pass through Macedonia and Achaia, then return to Jerusalem (19:21). *Ephesus; 56 A.D.* ★

192. Paul sent Timothy and Erastus to Corinth via Macedonia, while he remained in Ephesus (19:22; 1 Cor. 4:17). *Ephesus to Corinth, via Macedonia; 56 A.D.*

193. Paul wrote his letter now known as 1 Corinthians, and sent Titus to Corinth to deliver it to the Church there (2 Cor. 7:6-7, 13-15). *Ephesus to Corinth; 56 A.D.*

Note: **Delivering the First Epistle to the Corinthians**—Scholars have pieced together much of the detail of the writing of 1 Corinthians from scraps of information drawn from the two Corinthian epistles. It is asserted that Titus went by ship, and thus arrived earlier than Timothy, who traveled the less direct route by land.

Note: **The Second Group of Pauline Epistles**—This group consists of either three or four epistles: 1 Corinthians, 2 Corinthians, Galatians (if it was not written from Antioch seven years earlier, prior to the second missionary journey), and Romans. They probably were written between Easter, 55 A.D. and Easter, 57 A.D., during the latter half of Paul's third missionary journey. First Corinthians was written near the end of Paul's work in Ephesus; 2 Corinthians (and Galatians, if not previously written from Antioch) were written during his journey through Macedonia; Romans was written while Paul was at Corinth. The first group of epistles (1 and 2 Thessalonians) focuses on the second coming of Christ as the central theme. This second group has as its major message the reconciliation of man with God and with his fellow man through the atoning sacrifice of Jesus Christ.

194. Demetrius, a silversmith, agitated the other silversmiths against Paul, because in his preaching Paul taught that "they be no gods, which are made with hands." **Their complaint: their business of making silver shrines to the goddess Diana was being affected, and that Paul's preaching was causing the temple to Diana to be "despised" (19:23-28).** *Ephesus; 56 A.D.* ★

Note: **The Goddess Diana**—Diana was the Roman goddess of the moon, and was usually represented as a virgin huntress. The inhabitants of Ephesus, centuries earlier, took over the shrine of an Anatolian fertility goddess, the Semitic goddess Ashtoreth, patroness of the sexual instinct. The Greeks worshipped her under the name of Artemis, goddess of the hunt, the wild, of fertility and childbearing. The Greek representation of the goddess was a grotesque image of a woman with a turreted head and many breasts. Like the worship of Aphrodite at Corinth, worship of Diana involved sexual relations with the priestess courtesans of the temple located outside the city. The linking of the Roman goddess Diana with the Greek goddess Artemis is considered erroneous today.

195. The whole city rushed into the theater. They caught three converts: Gaius, Aristarchus, and Alexander. Aroused, the people chanted "great is Diana of the Ephesians" for two hours (19:29-34). *Ephesus; 56 A.D.*

196. The town clerk finally appeased the people, telling Demetrius and the craftsmen to place their charges in a lawful assembly. He warned that they were in danger of being questioned (by the Romans) for their spontaneous gathering, and eventually dismissed them (19:35-41). *Ephesus; 56 A.D.*

197. Paul and his companions were "pressed out of measure," so that they "dispaired even of life" and "had the sentence of death," but were delivered by God (2 Cor. 1:8-10). *Ephesus; 56 A.D.*(?). ★

Note: **The Time of Paul's Deliverance from Death**—The allusion given by Paul in 2 Corinthians to this time of great danger does not tell what event he is describing, nor the time nor sequence in which it occurred. It is also uncertain if it has reference to danger from others or from illness. It would appear, however, that it occurred during Paul's stay in Ephesus. On this or some other occasion Priscilla and Aquila "laid down their own necks," or risked their life in Paul's behalf (Rom. 16:2-3). Paul speaks of repeated imprisonments in 2 Corinthians 11:23, and in Romans he speaks of Andronicus and Junia, who had been imprisoned with him (Rom. 16:7). It is assumed that one or more of these imprisonments must have occurred during his stay in Ephesus during his third missionary journey. The most likely time for such a circumstance is after the agitation of the silversmiths. He also tells of having "many adversaries" (1 Cor. 16:9) and of being in "jeopardy every hour" so severe that he comments, "I die daily" (1 Cor. 15:30-31).

198. Paul came to Troas. Not finding Titus, he moved on toward Macedonia (2 Cor. 3:12-13). *Ephesus to Troas, toward Macedonia; 56 A.D.*

199. Paul apparently was troubled with some type of illness or bodily suffering during this period (2 Cor. 4:16-5:10; Rom. 8:18). *Traveling through Macedonia; 56 A.D.*

200. In Macedonia Paul finally was joined by Titus, who was returning from carrying Paul's epistle (1 Corinthians) to Corinth (2 Cor. 7:5-6). *Macedonia; 56 A.D.*

201. Paul went through Macedonia, and gave much exhortation to the Church there (20:1-2). *Macedonia; fall, 56 A.D.*

Note: **Paul's Trip Through Macedonia**—This journey probably took him to Philippi, Neapolis, Amphipolis, Apollonia, Thessalonica, and Berea, where the gospel previously had been preached, and possibly to other cities.

Note: **Alternate Time for the Writing of Galatians**—Scholars are divided on the time of the writing of the epistle to the Galatians. If not written prior to Paul's second missionary journey, it may have been written at this time. Others believe it was written from Ephesus prior to the writing of 1 Corinthians. There is no evidence sufficiently definitive to resolve the matter with finality.

202. Paul wrote his letter now known as 2 Corinthians. He sent Titus, with two other men, to Corinth to deliver it (2 Cor. 8:16-24; 12:18). Titus was also to collect money for the poor saints in Jerusalem (2 Cor. 8:1-8). *Macedonia; fall, 56 A.D.*

Note: **Paul's Revised Plan for Visiting Corinth**—In 1 Cor. 16:5-6, Paul indicated his intent to pass through Macedonia on his way to Corinth, and then to spend the winter in that city. This was a revision of his original plan, mentioned in 2 Cor. 1:15-16;

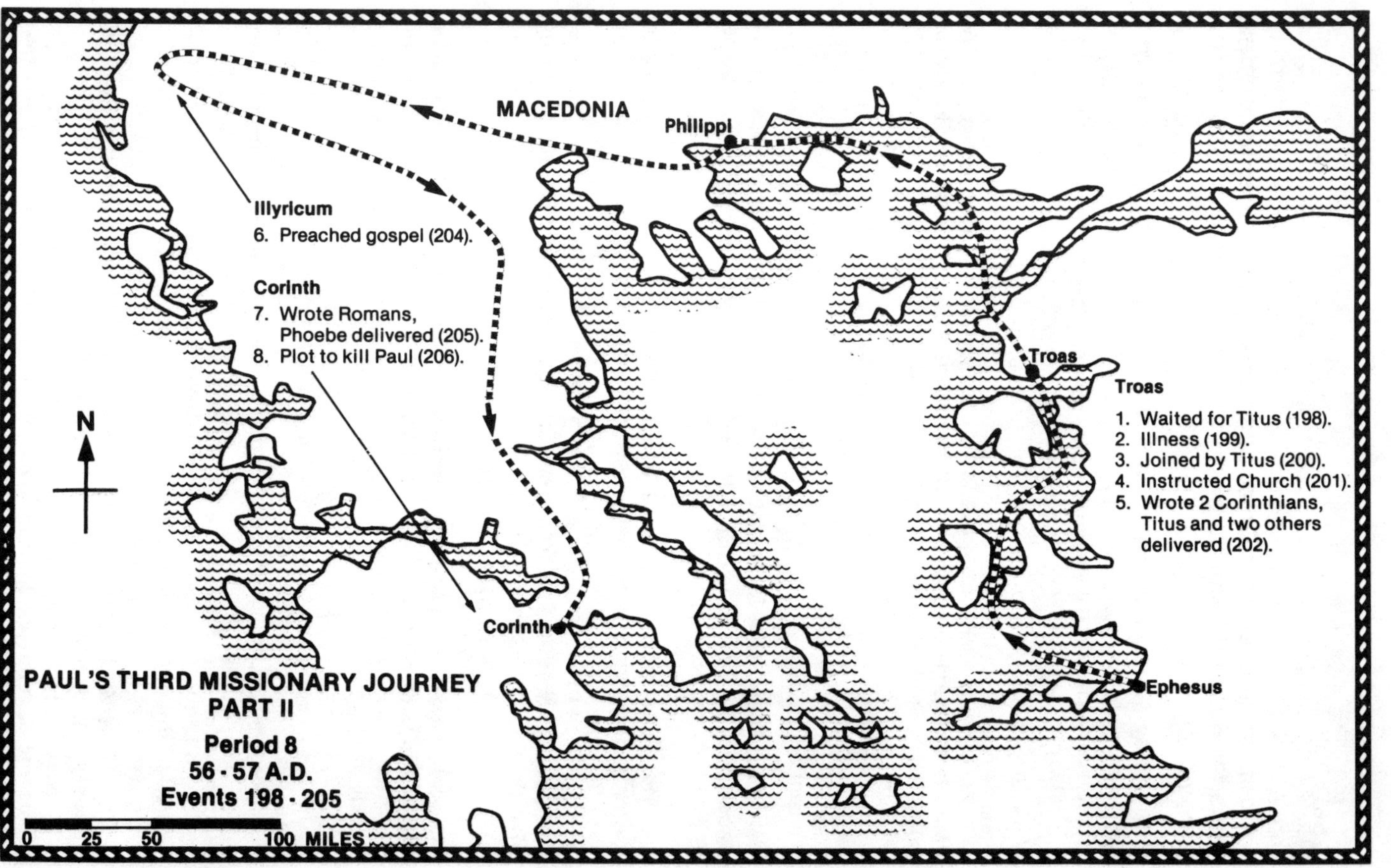
MACEDONIA
Philippi
Illyricum
6. Preached gospel (204).
Corinth
7. Wrote Romans,
Phoebe delivered (205).
8. Plot to kill Paul (206).
Troas
Troas
1. Waited for Titus (198).
2. Illness (199).
3. Joined by Titus (200).
4. Instructed Church (201).
5. Wrote 2 Corinthians,
Titus and two others
delivered (202).
N
Corinth
Ephesus
PAUL'S THIRD MISSIONARY JOURNEY
PART II
Period 8
56 - 57 A.D.
Events 198 - 205
0 25 50 100 MILES

16:5-8, which was to sail to Corinth, then visit Macedonia and return to Corinth again, leaving Ephesus in the spring, after Pentecost.

203. Paul came into Greece and abode there for three months, primarily at Corinth and Cenchrea (20:3). *Macedonia to Corinth and surrounding areas; fall, 56 A.D.—winter, 57 A.D.*

204. Paul preached the gospel at Illyricum (Rom. 15:19). The time of this journey is unknown. It is believed to have occurred at this point in Paul's third missionary journey because this is the only unidentified period when he was in the general location. *Corinth to Illyricum to Corinth; winter, 57 A.D.*(?).

205. Paul wrote his epistle to the Romans. It was carried to the Church at Rome by Phoebe, a member of the Church at Cenchrea (Rom. 16:1-2). *Corinth; winter, 57 A.D.*

***Note:* Cenchreae**—This was the eastern harbor for Corinth, located about seven miles east of Corinth on the Saronic Gulf. It was a small village, and the only purpose of the area was to transport goods to Corinth which had arrived by sea.

206. Paul prepared to sail back to Syria, but suddenly changed his route and went back into Macedonia when Jewish opponents laid in wait for him at Corinth. He traveled to Philippi (20:3, 6). *Corinth to Philippi; spring, 57 A.D.*

***Note:* The Plot to Kill Paul**—It appears that the Jews planned to slay Paul en route to Troas, on board the Jewish pilgrim ship on which he had taken passage. Paul, apparently, went by land to Philippi while his companions traveled on the ship.

207. Paul sailed from Philippi after the days of unleavened bread, and came to Troas in five days (20:6). *Philippi to Troas; spring, 57 A.D.*

208. Paul joined his companions who waited for him at Troas. These included Sopater (from Berea), Aristarchus and Secundus (from Thessalonica), Gaius and Timothy (from Derbe), Tychicus and Trophimus (from Asia), and Luke (20:4-5). *Troas; spring, 57 A.D.*

***Note:* Luke**—Again, as in Acts 16:10-18, the account switches from the third person to "us" in the first person, indicating that Luke was traveling with the party. He continued with them all the way to Jerusalem (20:5-21:18).

209. Paul stayed seven days in Troas. He preached to the disciples until daybreak. A young man, Eutychus, went to sleep and fell from the loft. He was taken up dead, but Paul embraced him and brought him back to life (20:6-12). *Troas; spring, 57 A.D.* ★

210. Paul went on foot to Assos, while the others sailed there on a ship (20:13-14). *Troas to Assos; spring, 57 A.D.*

***Note:* Assos**—This town, a seaport of Mysia in Asia Minor, stood on a hill 770 feet high, overlooking the Gulf of Adramyttium. It was well fortified to resist invasions. Paul walked the 20 Roman miles to Assos while the ship sailed from Troas around Cape Lectum.

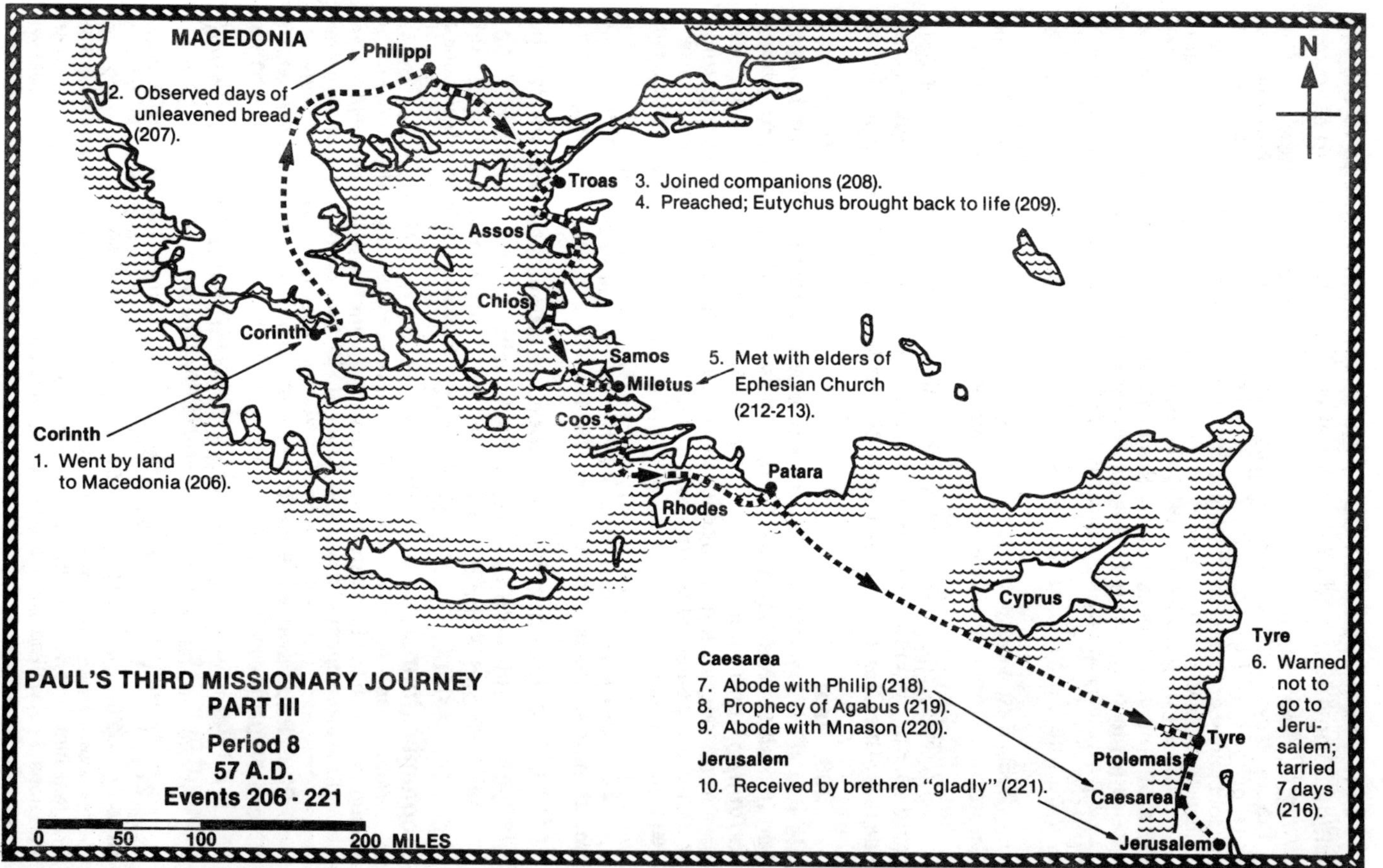
MACEDONIA
Philippi
2. Observed days of unleavened bread (207).
Troas
3. Joined companions (208).
4. Preached; Eutychus brought back to life (209).
Assos
Chios
Corinth
Samos
Miletus
5. Met with elders of Ephesian Church (212-213).
Coos
Corinth
1. Went by land to Macedonia (206).
Patara
Rhodes
Cyprus
N
Tyre
6. Warned not to go to Jeru-salem; tarried 7 days (216).
Caesarea
7. Abode with Philip (218).
8. Prophecy of Agabus (219).
9. Abode with Mnason (220).
Jerusalem
10. Received by brethren "gladly" (221).
Tyre
Ptolemais
Caesarea
Jerusalem
PAUL'S THIRD MISSIONARY JOURNEY
PART III
Period 8
57 A.D.
Events 206 - 221
0 50 100 200 MILES

211. The group sailed down the coast, from Mitylene to Chios, Samos, Trogyllium, and then to Miletus (20:14-15). *Assos to Miletus; spring, 57 A.D.*

Note: **Mitylene, Chios, Samos, Trogyllium, and Miletus**—*Mitylene* was the capital of the isle of Lesbos. The city was a center of Greek culture, and had an lent double harbor. *Chios* was a large island in the Aegean Sea opposite the Ionian peninsula in Asia Minor. The main city on the island was also named Chios, and was a Greek culture center—supposedly the birthplace of Homer. *Samos* was another island in the northeast Aegean Sea, with mountains rising over 5,000 feet. It was an important center of science and art, and a place known for luxurious living. *Trogyllium* is a slendor promontory jutting out to the southwest from the Asian mainland north of Miletus, which overlaps the eastern extension of Samos, leaving a strait between the two less than a mile wide. *Miletus* was an Ionian coastal city 36 miles south of Ephesus. It was a great sea port, though it was less prominent in Paul's day than Ephesus. Silt from the nearby river filled its harbor, and it is now more than five miles from the sea. The ruins of the city are today called Palatia.

212. Paul, anxious to be in Jerusalem on the day of Pentecost, decided not to visit Ephesus. He sent to Ephesus and asked the elders of the Church to meet with him at Miletus (20:16-17). *Miletus; spring, 57 A.D.*

213. Paul's farewell to the Ephesian Church: "I have taught you . . . repentance toward God, and faith toward our Lord Jesus Christ. . . . Take heed . . . after my departing shall grievous wolves enter in among you, not sparing the flock" **(20:18-38).** *Miletus; spring, 57 A.D. [★ —Major Discourse #8]*

Note: **Paul's Later Visit to the Ephesus Area**—Paul, at this time, apparently believed that the time of his death might be near, and did not think that he would ever return to the area. His life, though, was spared for many years and he later revisited Miletus (2 Tim. 4:20) and Ephesus (1 Tim. 1:3, 3:14).

214. The group sailed to Coos, Rhodes, and Patara (21:1). *Miletus to Patara; spring, 57 A.D.*

Note: **Coos, Rhodes, Patara**—*Coos* is a long, narrow island off the coast of Caria in southern Asia Minor. It was a fertile and productive area which produced wines, wheat, ointments and silk. *Rhodes* is a larger island, encompassing about 420 square miles. It was a free city, though little more than a provincial town. It was the center of a sun cult, and a 105-foot statue to the sun god once stood at the harbor entrance, though it had been toppled by an earthquake before Paul's time. *Patara* was an important seaport of Lycia near the mouth of the Xanthus River. It drew its prominence as a seaport from the trade coming from the river valley, and from the favorable position it occupied as the prevailing autumn winds brought ships there which were en route to Phoenicia or Egypt.

215. The group found a ship sailing for Phoenicia. They sailed past Cyprus and landed at Tyre (21:2-3). *Patara to Tyre; spring, 57 A.D.*

Note: **Phoenicia and Tyre**—The native name for Phoenicia was *Kenaan* (Canaan), meaning "lowland," as contrasted with the adjoining *Aram*, or highland (the Hebrew word for Syria). The area was a coastal plain about 28 miles long, with a width of 2 to 5 miles between the sea and the mountains to the east. The Greeks gave the area the name *Phoenicia*, meaning "palm tree." In New Testament times, the area was part of the Roman province of Syria, so its inhabitants were, at the same time, Canaanites, Syrians, and Phoenicians. *Tyre* was a major Phoenician port city which was larger than Jerusalem in New Testament times. It was first built on the mainland, then rebuilt on a nearby island. It was powerful as a merchant city and was especially famous for the metalwork, glassware and dyes which were produced there.

216. Disciples at Tyre told Paul through the Spirit not to go to Jerusalem. The group remained with them seven days (21:4-6). *Tyre; spring, 57 A.D.* ★

217. The group sailed from Tyre to Ptolemais, then on to Caesarea (21:6-8). *Tyre to Caesarea; spring, 57 A.D.*

Note: **Ptolemais**—This city was originally called *Acco.* It is situated on the coast of Israel, eight miles north of the promontory of Carmel, and thirty miles south of Tyre. It is now called *Acre.*

218. At Caesarea, the group entered the home of Philip and tarried there many days (21:8-9). *Caesarea; spring, 57 A.D.*

219. Agabus, a prophet from Judea, came and prophesied that the Jews at Jerusalem would bind Paul and deliver him to the Gentiles (21:10-14). *Caesarea; spring, 57 A.D.* ★

220. The group went in carriages to Jerusalem, accompanied by disciples from Caesarea. They lodged en route in the home of Mnason, an old disciple from Cyprus (21:15-16). *Caesarea to Jerusalem; spring, 57 A.D.*

221. The brethren at Jerusalem received Paul and his companions "gladly" (21:17). *Jerusalem; spring, 57 A.D.*

APPROXIMATE DISTANCES TRAVELED BY PAUL DURING HIS THIRD MISSIONARY JOURNEY

From	*To*	*Miles Traveled*
Syrian Antioch	Cilician Gates	140
Cilician Gates	Derbe	100
Derbe	Lystra	30
Lystra	Iconium	30
Iconium	Pisidian Antioch	85
Pisidian Antioch	Galatia and Phrygia	200+
Galatia and Phrygia	Ephesus	225
Ephesus	Troas	150
Troas	Macedonia	150
Macedonia	Greece	150+
Greece	Philippi	150+
Philippi	Troas	140
Troas	Assos	20
Assos	Mitylene	40
Mitylene	Chios	70
Chios	Samos	70
Samos	Miletus	50
Miletus	Cos	40
Cos	Rhodes	85
Rhodes	Patara	70
Patara	Tyre	400+
Tyre	Ptolemais	25
Ptolemais	Caesarea	30
Caesarea	Jerusalem	65
		2,515+

Period 9

PAUL'S TRIALS IN JERUSALEM AND CAESAREA

57 A.D. to 60 A.D.

Acts 21:18 to 26:32

Paul is Seized by a Mob in the Temple
Paul's Defense—the Account of His Conversion
Paul's Confrontation with the Sanhedrin
The Lord Appears to Paul
The Romans Move Paul to Caesarea to Prevent His Assassination
Paul's Defense Before Felix
Paul Appeals to Caesar
Paul's Defense Before Agrippa and Festus

222. Paul met with James and the elders of the Church, accompanied by those who accompanied him on his return from his third missionary journey. He declared what God had wrought among the Gentiles by his ministry, and the elders glorified God (21:18-20). *Jerusalem; spring, 57 A.D.* ★

223. Efforts of the Church at Jerusalem to avoid criticisms of the Jews. The elders, knowing the Jews were aware Paul had taught his Jewish converts it was no longer necessary to obey the law of Moses, counseled him to appear to be still obedient to that law. They instructed him to accompany four men (who had shaved their heads as a sign they had made a vow to God) to undergo the purification ritual, and enter into the temple, to show that he "also walkest orderly, and keepest the law" **(21:20-25).** *Jerusalem; spring 57 A.D.* ★

Note: **Rituals to End a Nazarite Vow**—It should be recalled that near the end of Paul's second missionary journey he made a vow (see Acts 18:18), which required the shaving of his head, and entry into the temple at Jerusalem at the completion of his vow. It appears that the elders at Jerusalem were asking Paul to undergo the same ritual at the end of his third missionary journey. The ritual is outlined in Numbers 6:13-21. It required the offering of a male lamb as a burnt offering, a female lamb as a sin offering, and a ram as a peace offering, plus the bringing of a basket of unleavened bread, cakes, and wafers to the priest. The individual also had to again shave his head, and put the hair in the fire under the sacrifices.

224. Paul went with the four men, and was seen in the temple almost seven days. Jews from Asia recognized him there and cried out against him. A mob formed. They drew Paul out of the temple and the doors were shut (21:26-30). *Jerusalem temple; spring, 57 A.D.*

225. The mob beat Paul and was about to kill him when Roman soldiers intervened. Paul was arrested, placed in chains, and taken to the stairs of the castle. The multitude followed, shouting "Away with him." **Paul obtained permission from the Roman chief captain to speak to the people, and addressed them in Hebrew (21:31-40).** *Jerusalem temple and Antonia fortress; spring, 57 A.D.*

Note: **The Antonia Fortress**—This fortification was connected with the temple at Jerusalem. It was built by Antiochus IV, but rebuilt by Herod the Great and named in honor of Mark Anthony, Herod's patron. The building was so large it had the form of a palace. The entire structure resembled that of a tower, but it also had towers at each of its four corners which were about 75 feet high. The tower on the southeast corner, which overlooked the temple, was 105 feet high. On the corner which adjoined the temple, two passages connected the fortress with the cloisters of the temple. A wide moat on the north separated the fortress from the rocky hill of Bezetha.

Note: **The Egyptian Rebel**—In Paul's day the extreme faction of the Zealot party were called "Sicarii," or assassins. These men engaged in "patriotic assassination," slaying influential Jews who were friendly to the Romans. Josephus tells of an Egyptian false prophet who led a group of 30,000 revolutionaries through the wilderness to the Mount of Olives, with the intent of storming the city of Jerusalem. The Romans, under Felix, disbursed them, but the Egyptian leader escaped (*Jewish War* II. 13.3-5; *Antiquities* XX.8.6).

Note: **Claudius Lysias**—Acts 23:26-30 records a letter from the chief captain, in which he is identified as Claudius Lysias. He was the tribune of the Roman cohort stationed at the Antonia fortress. His family name indicates that he was Greek, and his first name indicates that he had been adopted into the Claudian clan. He indicated to Paul that he had purchased his Roman citizenship for a large sum. Other than these few items, nothing else is known about the man except what Luke reveals in the Book of Acts.

226. Paul's defense—the account of his conversion: "The God of our fathers hath chosen thee, that thou shouldest know his will, and see that Just One, . . . for thou shalt be his witness unto all men of what thou hast seen and heard" **(22:1-21).** *Antonia Fortress in Jerusalem; the same day, spring, 57 A.D.* ***[★ —Major Discourse #9]***

Note: **Gamaliel**—This man, a doctor of the law, a Pharisee and grandson of Hillel, was regarded as one of the most distinguished Jewish teachers during his day. During the time of both Jesus and Paul he was a member of the Sanhedrin. He was more tolerant than other Pharisees of his day, and emphasized the human side of the law, stressing tolerance for others who were not Jews, voicing concern for women in connection with divorce laws, and relaxing the interpretation of Sabbath-day observance laws. Acts 5:34-40 records his words of caution to the Sanhedrin as he spoke in behalf of the disciples in the earliest days of the Church following the ascension of the Savior.

227. When the mob interrupted Paul, the chief captain commanded that he be brought into the castle and examined by scourging. The Romans stopped when Paul declared that he was a Roman citizen (21:22-29). *Antonia fortress in Jerusalem; the same day, spring, 57 A.D.*

228. The Roman chief captain commanded the chief priests and the Sanhedrin to assemble, and had Paul confront them so he could determine if the Jews had made a valid accusation against

Paul (22:30). *Antonia fortress in Jerusalem; the next day, spring, 57 A.D.*

229. When Ananias the high priest commanded the guards to strike him, Paul rebuked him, saying "Sittest thou to judge me after the law, and commandest me to be smitten contrary to the law?" **(23:1-5).** *In Jerusalem; the same day, spring, 57 A.D.* ★

***Note:* Ananias, the High Priest**—Ananias was the son of Nebedaeus, and a Sadducee. He held the office of high priest from 47 to 59 A.D. when he was deposed. In 52 A.D. he was sent by the legate of Syria because of his conduct in a dispute with the Samaritans, but he was able to regain his freedom and return to Palestine through the aid of Herod Agrippa II. His covetousness, insolence, and violent nature were notorious during his reign as high priest. Even after his term as high priest ended he exercised great power because of his wealth and his friendship with the Romans. The Sicarii assassinated him when the Jewish War began (66 or 67 A.D.).

230. Dissention broke out between the Sadducees and Pharisees when Paul said he was a Pharisee called in question about the doctrine of the resurrection. Paul was taken back to the castle (23:6-10). *In Jerusalem to Antonia fortress; the same day, spring, 57 A.D.* ★

***Note:* Conflicting Beliefs About Resurrection**—Paul apparently sought to divide the Sanhedrin by emphasizing a major doctrinal difference between its antagonistic factions. The Sadducees, the smaller party but the party of the high priests and the ruling class, did not believe in resurrection, but this was a major tenet of the Pharisees. The doctrinal question had been argued for years between the two factions. The row became so violent that the Roman commander had to intervene and take Paul back to the barracks.

231. The Lord appeared to Paul, saying, "Be of good cheer, Paul: for as thou hast testified of me in Jerusalem, so must thou bear witness also at Rome" **(23:11).** *Antonia fortress in Jerusalem; the next night, spring, 57 A.D.* ★

232. A group of more than 40 Jews banded together and vowed to assassinate Paul. They plotted with the chief priests to have Paul summoned the next day so they could ambush him. Paul's nephew exposed the plot to Paul and to the Roman chief captain (23:12-22). *Antonia fortress in Jerusalem; the next day, spring, 57 A.D.*

***Note:* "Sicarii," or Assassins**—Many believe that those who plotted to kill Paul were of the extremist element of the Zealots, called Sicarii. These assassins sought to slay prominent Jews they believed to be friends of Rome rather than Jewish nationalists.

233. Paul was taken under heavy Roman guard to Caesarea, where he was detained in Herod's judgment hall by Felix the governor (23:23-35). *Jerusalem to Antipatris to Caesarea; spring, 57 A.D.*

***Note:* Roman Army Organization**—The force assembled to conduct Paul to Caesarea was a substantial one. In the Roman army, a "Centurion" was a legionary officer who commanded a "century" composed of 50 to 100 infantrymen. He was roughly equivalent to a modern captain (though in social status was more like a non-commissioned officer). A "century" was a hundredth part of a legion, though in New Testament times Roman legions had only about 6,000 infantrymen, together with complements of other arms. A legion's infantry was divided into ten cohorts of 600 men, commanded by a "tribune." During Paul's time, the Roman army had 25 legions,

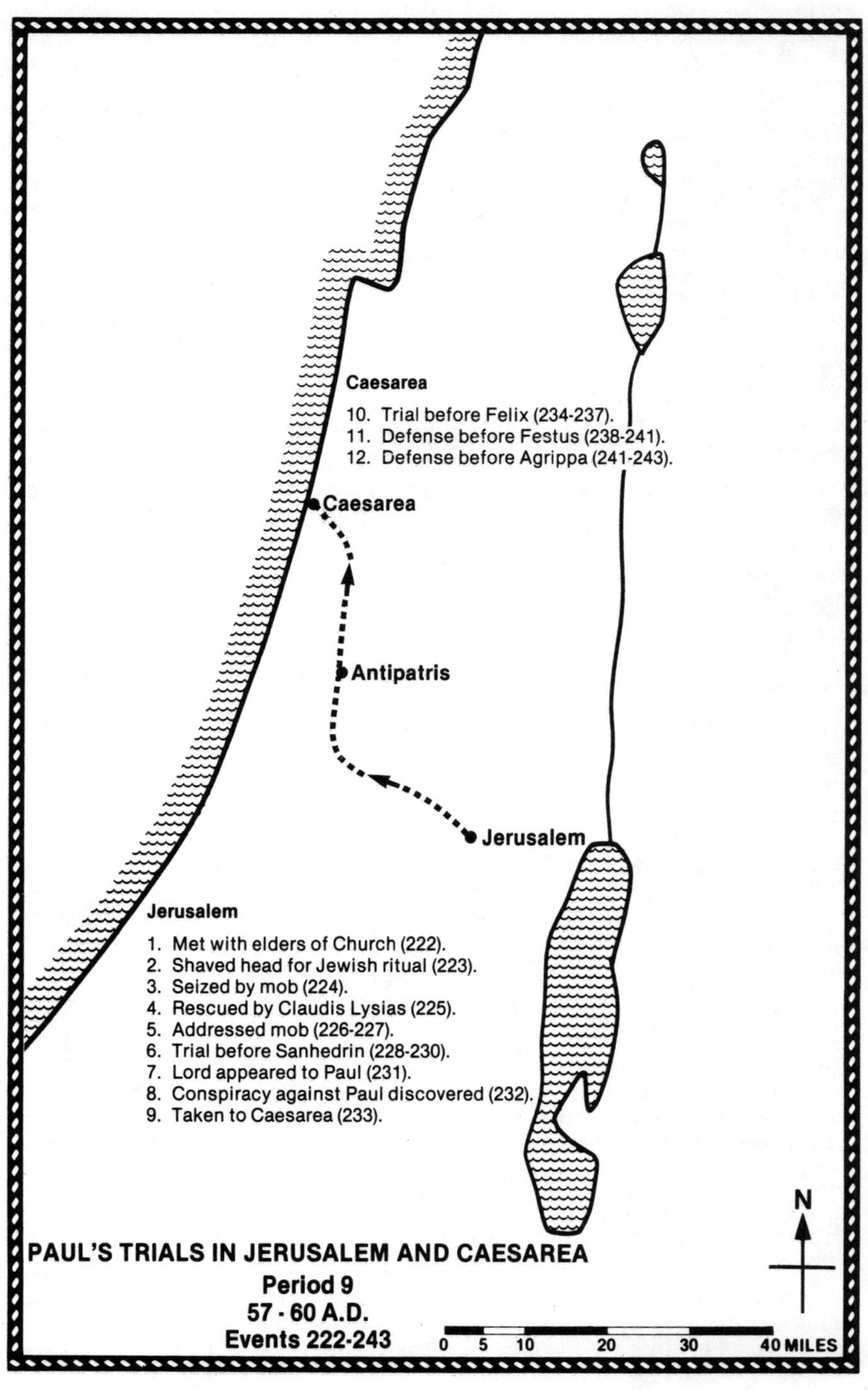

PAUL'S TRIALS IN JERUSALEM AND CAESAREA
Period 9
57 - 60 A.D.
Events 222-243

4 of which were stationed in Syria and Palestine. Soldiers from local areas were used to supplement the Roman forces.

Note: **Felix**—Antonius Felix served as the Roman procurator of Judaea from approximately 52 to 60 A.D. He was originally assigned only to Samaria, but in 52 A.D. his commission was enlarged to include all of Palestine except four Galilean cities assigned to Agrippa II. He was an ex-slave, probably Greek, and was one of the new bureaucracy of freemen whom the emperor Claudius used extensively to govern his affairs. His brother, Pallas, was Claudius' financial secretary and one of three powerful freemen who administered the Roman government. He may have been the source of Felix's appointment. He was ruthless in his suppression of the Zealots, and crucified many of them. His cruelty in his administration goaded the Jewish nation into rebellion against Rome, and brought about the rise of the Sicarii, or political assassins, who slew many of the Jewish leaders friendly to Felix including Jonathan, the high priest whose recommendation had led to Felix's appointment. Tacitus said of him that "he revelled in cruelty and lust, and wielded the power of a king with the mind of a slave."

Note: **Antipatris**—This town was founded by Herod the Great and named in honor of his father, Antipater. It was on the road from Lydda to Caesarea, and has been identified with the present site of Ras-el-'Ain.

234. Ananias, the high priest, and other elders came to Caesarea. Tertullus, an orator, stated their charges against Paul: "We have found this man a pestilent fellow, and a mover of sedition among all the Jews throughout the world, and a ringleader of the sect of the Nazarenes. . . ." **(24:1-9).** *Jerusalem to Caesarea; five days later, spring, 57 A.D.*

235. Paul's defense before Felix: "After the way which they call heresy, so worship I the God of my fathers, . . . herein do I exercise myself, to have always a conscience void of offense toward God, and toward men" **(24:10-21).** *Caesarea; the same day, spring, 57 A.D.* ***[★ —Major Discourse #10]***

236. Felix deferred the matter, and had Paul detained but with liberty to be visited by others (24:22-23). *Caesarea; spring, 57 A.D.*

237. Paul met frequently with Felix for two years, and "reasoned of righteousness, temperance, and judgment to come" **(24:24-27).** *Caesarea; 57-59 A.D.* ★

Note: **Drusilla**—The third wife of the Roman procurator Felix, Drusilla was the youngest of the three daughters of Herod Agrippa I, and was born about 37 A.D. It is believed that Felix seduced her while she was the wife of Azizus, king of Emesa (modern Homs). She apparently taught Felix much about Jewish life and customs.

Note: **Possible Time of Writing of Paul's Third Group of Epistles**—During the more than two years Paul spent at Caesarea, it is possible that he composed his third group of epistles, which consists of Philippians, Colossians, Ephesians, and Philemon. Some scholars hold to this view, citing passages such as Philip. 1:13: "My bonds in Christ are manifest in all the palace, . . ." and pointing out that at Caesarea he was confined in Herod's palace (judgment hall: Acts 23:35). The more common view, however, is that the four epistles were written from Rome. ("They of Caesar's household," Philip. 4:22, suggests Rome.)

238. Felix was replaced as governor by Porcius Festus. Paul remained a prisoner (24:27). *Caesarea; 60 A.D.*

Note: **Porcius Festus**—Festus became procurator about 60 A.D., and served until his death in 62 A.D. He is believed to have been less tyrannical than Felix in his methods of administering Rome's affairs in Palestine, though he still executed large numbers of Jewish patriots as he followed Felix's policy of curbing Messianism. He was able, however, to curb the Sicarii. His friendship for Agrippa II developed when he sided with him against the temple priesthood who built a wall so Agrippa could not view temple activities.

239. The chief priest and other Jews informed Festus about Paul. Festus had them come to Caesarea to state their grievances. Paul's reply: "Neither against the law of the Jews, neither against the temple, nor yet against Caesar, have I offended any thing at all" **(25:1-8).** *Jerusalem and Caesarea; 60 A.D.*

240. When Festus asked Paul if he would go to Jerusalem to be tried, Paul replied, "I stand at Caesar's judgment seat, where I ought to be judged . . . I appeal unto Caesar." **Festus announced that** "unto Caesar shalt thou go" **(25:9-12).** *Caesarea; 60 A.D.*

241. When King Agrippa and Bernice came to visit Festus at Caesarea, the governor told the king about Paul. The king agreed to hear Paul's defense. People assembled and Festus introduced Paul's case to the king (25:13-27). *Caesarea; 60 A.D.*

Note: **King Agrippa and Bernice**—*Marcus Julius Agrippa* was the son of Agrippa I and Cypros. He was only 17 when his father died in 44 A.D., so the emperor Claudius did not make him king of Palestine. In 50 A.D., when his uncle Herod, king of Chalcis died, he was given control over his tiny kingdom in the Lebanons. Then, in 53 A.D., he was given control over the territories formerly ruled by Philip the tetrarch, Lysanias, and Varus. He tried to convince the Jews not to revolt in 66 A.D., but was unsuccessful. He remained as the king of Chalcis until his death in 100 A.D. *Bernice*, his consort, was also his sister, and he lived with her in a criminal union. She was previously married, at age 13, to her uncle Herod, and bore him two sons. When he died she lived incestuously with Herod Agrippa II, then was married for a brief period to Polemo, the king of Cilicia, and later was also the mistress of Vespasian and Titus, who eventually cast her aside.

242. Paul's defense before Agrippa: Christ sent me as a minister and a witness unto the Gentiles, to turn them "from the power of Satan unto God, that they may receive forgiveness of sins, and inheritance among them which are sanctified by faith. . . ." **(26:1-29).** *Caesarea; 60 A.D.* ***[★ —Major Discourse #11]***

243. King Agrippa's response: "Almost thou persuadest me to be a Christian. . . . This man might have been set at liberty, if he had not appealed unto Caesar" **(26:28-32).** *Caesarea; 60 A.D.*

Period 10

PAUL'S FIRST IMPRISONMENT IN ROME

60 A.D. to 63 A.D.

Acts 27:1 to 28:16

Paul Travels to Rome with Aristarchus
Paul Prophesies Harm Will Come
Paul Prophesies All Lives Will Be Saved but the Ship Lost
The Ship Is Wrecked at Melita
Paul Is Bitten by a Poisonous Snake but Unharmed
Paul Heals the Father of Publius
Paul Lives in a Hired House Under Guard at Rome
Paul Explains His Bondage to the Jews
Paul Writes the "Captivity Epistles":
Colossians, Ephesians, Philemon and Philippians
Paul Is Released from Imprisonment After Two Years

244. Paul and other prisoners were sent to Rome. They were guarded by Julius, a Roman centurion, and his soldiers. Aristarchus traveled as Paul's companion (27:1-2). *Caesarea; fall, 60 A.D.*

Note: **Augustus' Band**—This was probably one of the five Roman cohorts which were stationed at Caesarea. A cohort was the ancient equivalent of a regiment. The cohorts were usually either 500 or 1000 men, and commanded by a prefect or a military tribune (rendered in the King James Version as "captain" or "chief captain.") "Augustus' band," meaning the "Emperor's own," was probably a title of honor, rather than a distinct identification of a specific unit.

Note: **Aristarchus**—Paul's traveling companion was "a Macedonian of Thessalonica" (Acts 19:29; 27:2), who was also a Jew (Col. 4:10-11). He accompanied Paul back to Jerusalem at the end of his third missionary journey, and apparently was with Paul as he traveled to Rome and was confined there (Col. 4:10; Philem. 23-24) along with Paul. Whether his confinement was voluntary or not is uncertain.

Note: **A Ship of Adramyttium**—This was a town of Mysia, in the Roman province of Asia, located on the Adramyttene Gulf. It was a place of considerable political and intellectual importance, and ships sailed throughout the Aegean and Mediterranean Seas from its harbor.

Note: **Travel on the Mediterranean Sea**—The detailed account of Paul's voyage to Rome stands as one of the best records available of sea travel in ancient times and thus has added historical significance.

245. The party sailed from Caesarea to Sidon, then south of Cyprus to Myra (27:1-5). *Caesarea to Myra; fall, 60 A.D.*

Note: **"Under Cyprus"**—West-bound ships would customarily sail in the lee of the island, on its east side, to shield themselves from the strong west winds.

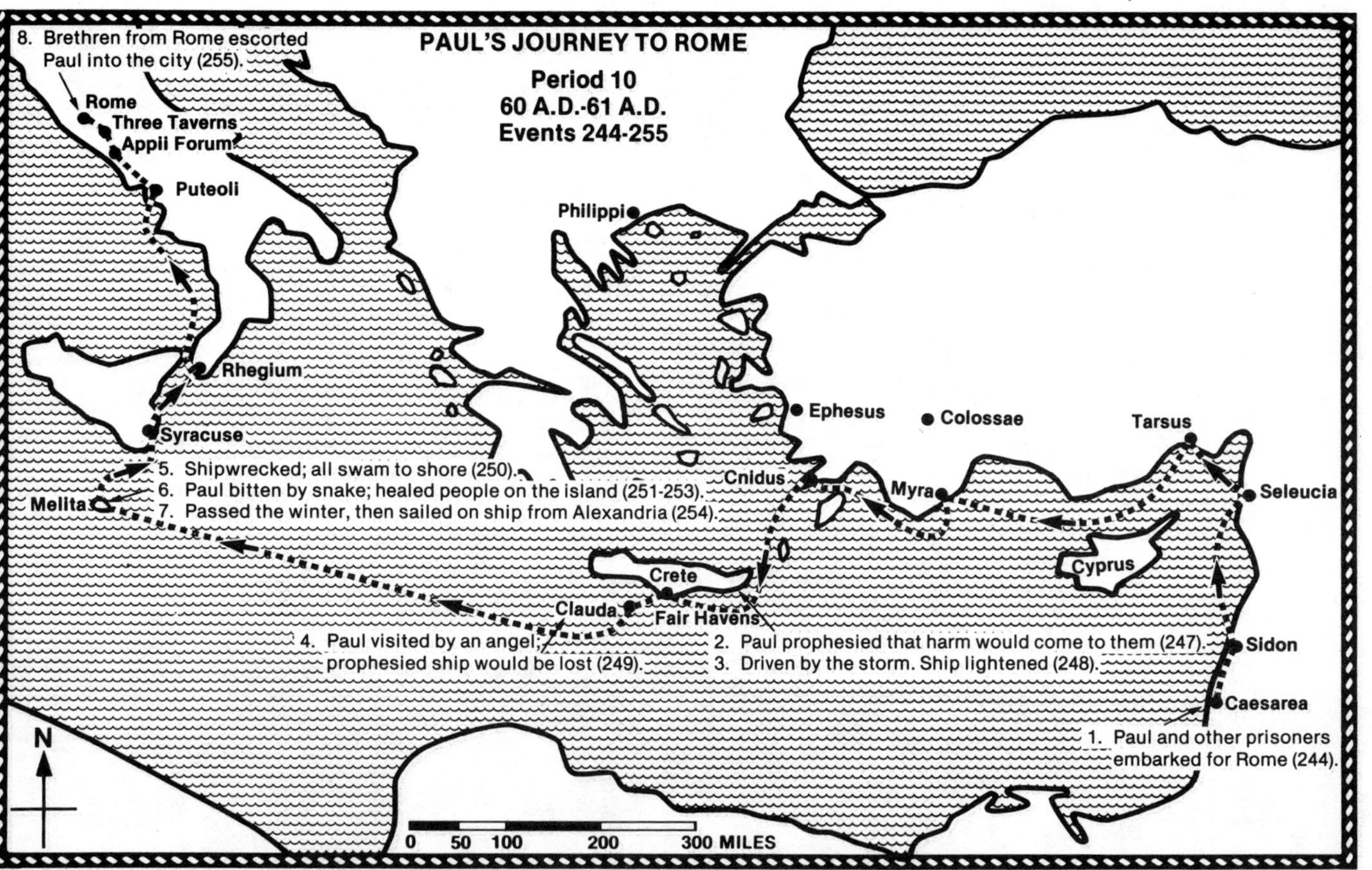
PAUL'S JOURNEY TO ROME
Period 10
60 A.D.-61 A.D.
Events 244-255
8. Brethren from Rome escorted Paul into the city (255).
Rome
Three Taverns
Appii Forum
Puteoli
Philippi
Rhegium
Syracuse
Ephesus
Colossae
Tarsus
Seleucia
Cnidus
Myra
Melita
5. Shipwrecked; all swam to shore (250).
6. Paul bitten by snake; healed people on the island (251-253).
7. Passed the winter, then sailed on ship from Alexandria (254).
Crete
Cyprus
Claudа
Fair Havens
4. Paul visited by an angel; prophesied ship would be lost (249).
2. Paul prophesied that harm would come to them (247).
3. Driven by the storm. Ship lightened (248).
Sidon
Caesarea
1. Paul and other prisoners embarked for Rome (244).
N
0 50 100 200 300 MILES

246. At Myra they changed to a ship from Alexandria bound for Italy. They sailed slowly, against the wind, past Cnidus, south of Crete, past Salmone to the Fair Havens (27:6-8). *Myra to Fair Havens; fall, 60 A.D.*

Note: **Myra**—This city was the dividing point between the south and west coasts of Asia Minor, which made it a natural point to transfer from ship to ship in order to sail in different directions. It was located on Cape Crio, and held the status of a free city.

Note: **Crete, Salmone and Fair Havens**—The island of *Crete*, 150 miles long and varying from 7 to 30 miles in breadth, is located about 60 miles south of Greece. Mountains on the island rise to 7,000 feet. The island is almost equal distance from Africa, Asia, and Europe, and is the home of very early civilizations. *Salmone* is the north-east promontory of the island, while *Fair Havens* is a harbor located on a small bay on the south coast of the island, near Lasea. To sail "under Crete" meant to sail to the east and south of the island in order to escape the force of the prevailing west winds.

Note: **The Fast**—The fast referred to was the Jewish Day of Atonement, which occurred about the time of the fall equinox. Ancient mariners had long known that the time of dangerous sailing was the two-month-long period from mid-September to mid-November, as winter approached. Almost all navigation was then suspended during the winter months, from mid-November until early March.

247. Paul advised the captain and centurion that the voyage was dangerous, and prophesied that harm would come to them (27:9-10). *Fair Havens, Crete; fall, 60 A.D.* ★

248. The captain attempted to sail to Phenice, to pass the winter there. They were caught by a storm and driven past the isle of Clauda. They lightened the ship and continued sailing, though they despaired of their lives (27:11-20). *South of Crete; fall, 60 A.D.*

Note: **Phenice, Clauda, and the Euroclydon Wind**—*Phenice* was a harbor on the isle of Crete, less than 50 miles west of Fair Havens. One half of the semi-circular harbor faced southwest, while the other half faced northwest; so the harbor afforded good protection from the northern winds. *Clauda*, or more correctly *Cauda*, is a small island about 23 miles south of Phenice. The wind *Euroclydon* (commonly called "Euraquilo") is an east-northeast tempestuous wind. The ship sailed to the south of Cauda, seeking shelter. The small row boat being towed at the stern of the ship filled with water in the sudden storm, and they experienced considerable difficulty in hauling it aboard. Broad straps were passed under the ship and pulled tight to hold the timbers together. They were afraid of being driven by the storm into the "Greater Syrtis," the quicksands which lay southwest of Cauda.

249. Paul prophesied that all lives would be saved but the ship would be lost and they would be cast up on an island. He told of receiving a visit from an angel (27:21-26). *South of Clauda; fall, 60 A.D.* ★

250. The ship was run aground on an island and broken up by the violent waves. The centurion allowed the prisoners, crew and soldiers to swim to shore. All 276 made it to land safely (27:27-44). *The Isle of Melita (now known as Malta); fourteen days after departing from Fair Havens, fall, 60 A.D.*

Note: **Melita (Malta)**—Almost 600 miles west of Crete lies the island of Malta, where Paul was shipwrecked. The ninety-five-square-mile island is about 60 miles south of Sicily. It is believed that the shipwreck occurred on the west side of the island at St. Paul's bay, eight miles from Valetta, and five miles from the old capital of Citta-Vecchia. The island's position made it an important commercial station from earliest times.

251. The inhabitants of the island of Melita cared for the shipwrecked survivors (28:1-2). *Melita (Malta); fall, 60 A.D.*

252. Paul was bitten by a poisonous snake while gathering firewood but was not harmed. The people said he was a god (28:3-6). *Melita (Malta); fall, 60 A.D.* ★

253. Paul laid hands on the sick father of Publius, the chief man of the island, and healed him. Others with diseases also came to him and were healed (28:7-10). *Melita (Malta); winter, 60-61 A.D.* ★

Note: **"Bloody Flux"**—This illness is usually believed to be dysentery. Malta was part of the province of Sicily, and Publius must have been a subordinate to the praetor of Sicily. Tradition places his home in Citta-Vecchia.

254. Three months later they set sail on an Alexandrian ship which had wintered on the isle. They sailed to Syracuse, then to Rhegium, and then to Puteoli where they spent a week with the brethren, then went on towards Rome (28:11-14). *Malta to Puteoli; spring, 61 A.D.*

Note: **Syracuse, Rhegium, and Puteoli**—*Syracuse*, located on the east coast of Sicily, was the most important city of the island. It was a Roman colony, and was about 100 miles north of Malta. *Rhegium* (now Reggio) is located on the southwest coast of Italy, close to the point of shortest passage from Sicily. This was an important harbor, and ships would wait there for favorable winds. During Paul's day the population was a mixture of Greek and Latin. *Puteoli* was an important harbor on the west coast of Italy, near Naples. It was a center for trade sailing to the east, and was Italy's corn mart which received ships from Alexandria in Egypt. Its modern name is Pozzuoli.

255. Brethren from Rome came and met the party at the Appii Forum, and the three taverns, and escorted them into the city (28:15). *Puteoli to Rome; spring, 61 A.D.*

Note: **The Appii Forum and Three Taverns**—The *Appii Forum*, or market of Appius, was 43 Roman miles south of Rome on the Appian Road. This route was the main line of communication and land transportation between Rome and the East. The *Three Taverns* were 10 Roman miles south of the city of Rome.

256. In Rome, Paul was allowed to live by himself with a soldier that kept him (28:16). *Rome; spring, 61 A.D.*

257. Paul explained his bondage to the chief of the Jews: "For the hope of Israel I am bound with this chain" **(28:17-22).** *Rome, at Paul's lodging; three days after Paul's arrival, spring, 61 A.D.* ★

258. Paul preached to the Jews at his lodging: "He expounded and testified the kingdom of God, persuading them concerning Jesus, both out of the law of Moses, and out of the prophets, from morning till evening" **(28:23-29).** *Rome, at Paul's lodging; a few days later, spring, 61 A.D.* ★

259. Paul dwelt two years in his own hired house, and received all who visited him, "Preaching the kingdom of God, and teaching those things which concern the Lord Jesus Christ, with all confidence, no man forbidding him" **(28:30-31).** *Rome, at Paul's house; 61-63 A.D.* ★

***Note:* The End of the Book of Acts**—At this point the formal account of the ministry of Paul and the other disciples ends. The rest of the events listed are pieced together from clues found in the various New Testament books, or from other historical sources. The dating becomes even less certain, and the details become more sparse.

260. Paul's preaching was "manifest in all the palace, and in all other places." **Because of Paul's presence in Rome, many of the brethren grew confident and became** "more bold to speak the word without fear" **(Philip. 1:12-14).** *Rome; 61-63 A.D.*

***Note:* Paul's Visitors and Fellow Workers in Rome**—In addition to the help and assistance of *Aristarchus*, his traveling companion, Paul was visited and attended by many friends and fellow-workers:

•*Luke*, the "beloved physician"—was present when Colossians, Ephesians, and Philemon were written (Col. 4:14; Philem. 24).

•*Demas*—was present when Colossians, Ephesians and Philemon were written (Col. 4:14; Philem. 24). He later forsook Paul, "having loved this present world," and went to Thessalonica (2 Tim. 4:10).

•*Timothy*—was present when Colossians, Ephesians, Philemon and Philippians were written (Col. 1:1; Philem. 1; Phil. 1:1). Paul sent him to Philippi shortly after the epistle to the Philippians was written (Phil. 2:19-30).

•*John Mark*—was present when Colossians, Ephesians and Philemon were written (Col. 4:10).

•*Tychicus*—"a faithful minister and fellowservant in the Lord" whom Paul sent to carry his epistles to the Colossians (Col. 4:7-9) and Ephesians (Eph. 6:21).

•*Epaphras*—"a faithful minister of Christ" who brought Paul news of the Colossian church (Col. 1:7-8).

•*Jesus*, called *Justus*—a Jewish member present when Colossians was written (Col. 4:11).

•*Onesimus*—"a brother beloved," a slave Paul converted (Philem. 10-16).

•*Epaphroditus*—brought money from the Church at Philippi (Philip. 4:14-18).

The previously written epistle to the Romans identifies numerous other Church members there: (Romans chapter 16)

•Priscilla and Aquila (previous acquaintances from Corinth: Acts 18:2ff)

•Epaenetus (the firstfruits of Achaia unto Christ)

•Mary (who bestowed much labor on us)

•Andronicus and Junia (my kinsmen, my fellowprisoners, of note among the apostles, in Christ before me)

•Amplias (my beloved in the Lord)

•Urbane (our helper in Christ)

•Stachys (my beloved)

•Apelles (approved in Christ)

•Aristobulus and his household

•Herodion (my kinsman)

•Narcissus and his household (which are in the Lord)

•Tryuphena and Tryphosa (who labour in the Lord)

•Persis (beloved, who labored much in the Lord)

•Rufus and his mother (chosen in the Lord)

•Asyncritus, Phlegon, Hermas, Patrobas, Hermes, and the brethren with them

•Philologus, Julia, Nereus and his sister, Olympas, and all the saints with them

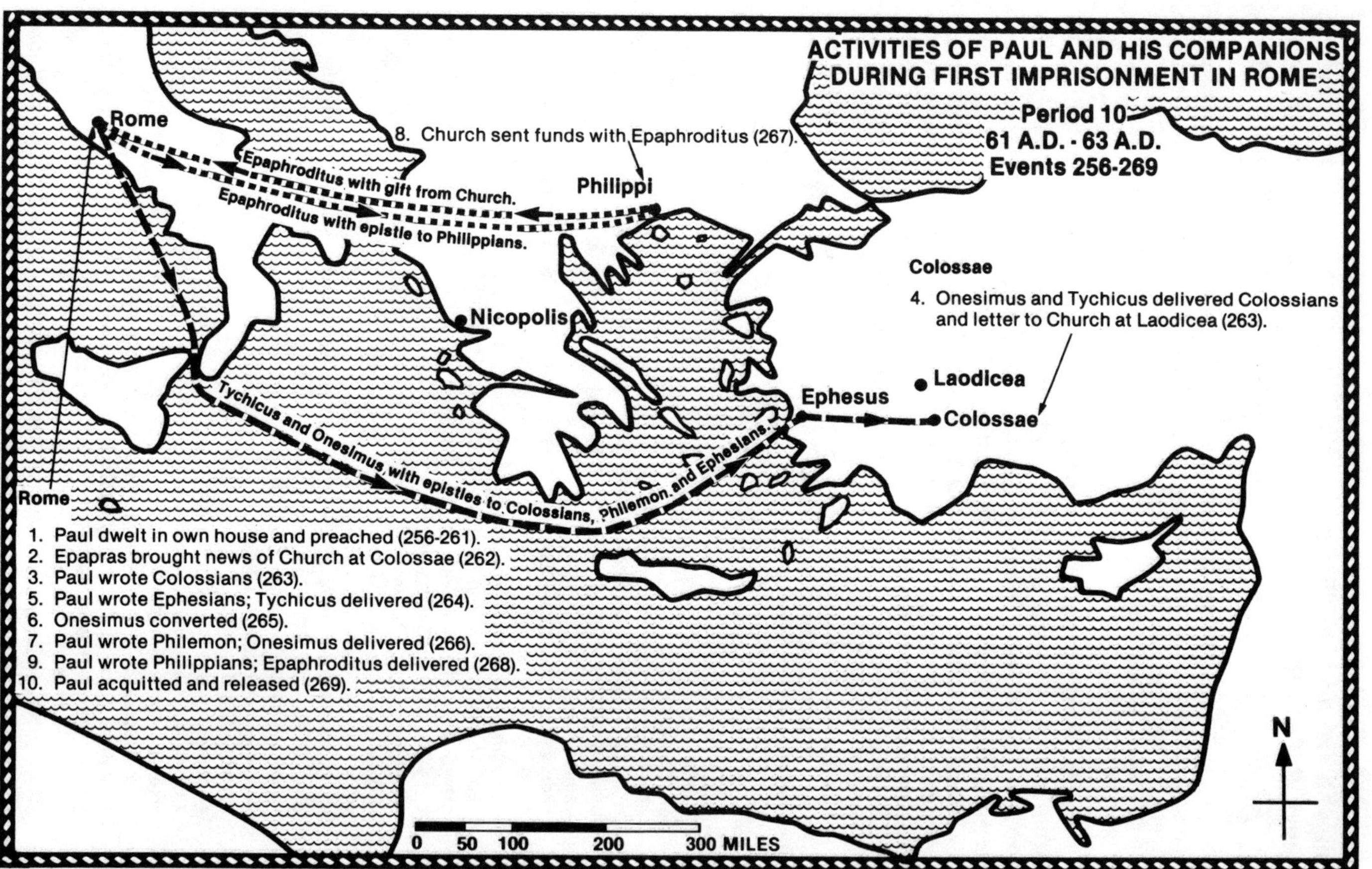
ACTIVITIES OF PAUL AND HIS COMPANIONS
DURING FIRST IMPRISONMENT IN ROME
Period 10
61 A.D. - 63 A.D.
Events 256-269
Rome
8. Church sent funds with Epaphroditus (267).
Epaphroditus with gift from Church.
Epaphroditus with epistle to Philippians.
Philippi
Nicopolis
Colossae
4. Onesimus and Tychicus delivered Colossians
and letter to Church at Laodicea (263).
Laodicea
Ephesus
Colossae
Tychicus and Onesimus, with epistles to Colossians, Philemon, and Ephesians.
Rome
1. Paul dwelt in own house and preached (256-261).
2. Epapras brought news of Church at Colossae (262).
3. Paul wrote Colossians (263).
5. Paul wrote Ephesians; Tychicus delivered (264).
6. Onesimus converted (265).
7. Paul wrote Philemon; Onesimus delivered (266).
9. Paul wrote Philippians; Epaphroditus delivered (268).
10. Paul acquitted and released (269).
N
0 50 100 200 300 MILES

261. The preaching of Christ became a matter of controversy in Rome. Some preached Christ "of envy and strife," **some** "of good will," **and some** "of contention, not sincerely, supposing to add affliction" **to Paul (Philip. 1:15-18).** *Rome; 61-63 A.D.*

262. Epapras brought news to Paul that false teachers had come into the Church at Colossae (Col. 2:8-23). (He probably brought news of the churches at Laodicea and Ephesus too.) *Colossae to Rome; 62 A.D.*

263. Paul wrote his epistle to the Colossians, and sent it with Onesimus and Tychicus (Col. 4:7-9). He also wrote a letter (now lost) to the Church at Laodicea (Col. 4:16). *Rome to Colossae and Laodicea; 62 A.D.*

Note: **The Captivity Epistles**—The third group of Pauline epistles were written during the two years of Paul's imprisonment in Rome. They are *Colossians, Ephesians, Philemon* and *Philippians.* Three of them (Colossians, Philemon and Ephesians) were sent by Paul at the same time:

- •Onesimus and Tychicus carried the epistle to the Colossians (Col. 4:7-9),
- •Onesimus carried the epistle to Philemon at Colossae, and
- •Tychicus carried the epistle to the Ephesians (Eph. 6:21).

There is disagreement whether Philippians was written before or after the other three letters.

264. Paul wrote his epistle to the Ephesians, and sent it with Tychicus (Eph. 6:21). *Rome to Ephesus; 62 A.D.*

Note: **Colossae and Laodicea**—These two cities are located 10 miles apart in Phrygia, in the Roman province of Asia. Colossae was originally of greater importance, but its influence dwindled as Laodicea grew and prospered. It was located in the upper valley of the Lycus River, about 10 miles east of Laodicea and 13 miles southeast of Hierapolis. Epaphras (Epaphroditus), a native of the city (Col. 4:12-13), had a great zeal for the churches in the three cities, and they formed a proselyting base for him, for Timothy, and for others. It appears that Paul himself never visited the city (Col. 2:1), though he was well acquainted with Philemon and his family, who lived there.

265. Paul converted Onesimus, a slave (Philem. 10). *Rome; 62 A.D.*

266. Paul wrote his epistle to Philemon, and sent it with Onesimus (Philem. 10-12). *Rome to Colossae; 62 A.D.*

Note: **Philemon and Onesimus**—*Philemon* was a well-to-do resident of Colossae. He was a member of the Church and owed his conversion to Paul (Philem. 19). *Onesimus* was a runaway slave who belonged to Philemon, who somehow made his way to Rome and was there converted to the gospel by Paul. The punishment for a slave's running away at that time was death. Paul's epistle was a request to Philemon that he not only take Onesimus back without punishment, but that he receive him "as a brother beloved" (Philem. 16). *Appia* was probably Philemon's wife, and *Archippus* his son. Tradition holds that Philemon became Bishop of Colossae, and that his family and Onesimus were martyred there during the Neronian persecution.

267. The Church at Philippi sent money to Paul to assist him during his imprisonment. The gift was brought by Epaphroditus,

who stayed at Rome to assist Paul (Phil. 4:14-18). *Philippi to Rome; 62 A.D.*

Note: **Epaphroditus**—Epaphroditus became "sick nigh unto death" while staying with Paul (Philip. 2:27), and then, after regaining his health, became homesick (Philip. 2:26). Paul sent him home, and had Epaphroditus carry his epistle to the Philippians (Philip. 2:25).

268. Paul wrote his epistle to the Philippians, and sent it with Epaphroditus (Philip. 2:25). *Rome to Philippi; 62 A.D.*

269. Paul was acquitted and released from confinement. *Rome; 63 A.D.*

Note: **The Roman Law Statute of Limitations**—Roman law prescribed a two-year period as the limit within which prosecutors had to come to Rome to present their case after an accused individual appealed to Caesar. It appears that the Jewish plaintiffs failed to come to Rome and the case was probably dropped by default. (Note that they didn't even notify the Jews in Rome that Paul was coming there. See Acts 28:21). The difficulty in assembling and bringing witnesses, and the great expense in time and money to travel to Rome, plus the weak legal basis for their case, probably influenced the decision of the Jewish leadership at Jerusalem not to pursue the case further. It is probable that Paul merely waited until the Roman equivalent of the statute of limitations had expired and then was released. His epistles clearly show that he expected to be set free (Philip. 1:25; 2:24; Philem. 22).

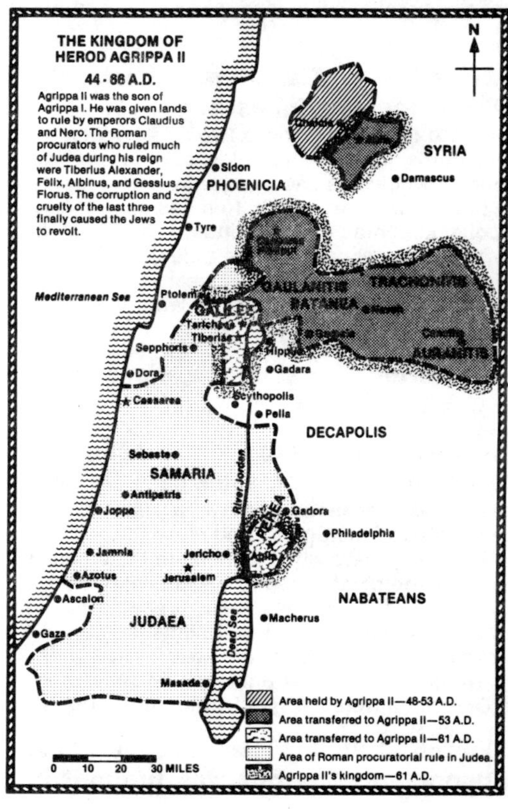

Period 11

PAUL'S FINAL JOURNEYS, IMPRISONMENT, AND MARTYRDOM

63 A.D. to 68 A.D.

1 Timothy, 2 Timothy, Titus, Hebrews

Paul's Visit to Macedonia and Asia
The Epistle to the Hebrews Is Written
Paul Journeys to Spain
Paul Preaches in the Ephesus Area with Timothy
Paul Takes Titus to Crete
Paul Spends the Winter in Nicopolis
Paul Writes First Timothy
Paul Writes Titus
Paul Is Arrested and Taken to Rome
Paul's First Hearing Before the Romans
Paul Writes Second Timothy
Paul Is Martyred by the Romans

Note: **The Order of Events in the Last Period of Paul's Life**—The events listed in this chapter are difficult to arrange in accurate chronological order because almost all of them are based on very fragmentary information. Nevertheless, they are significant events which should not be overlooked, and therefore are included here. Dates provided, of course, are approximations at best.

270. Paul journeyed to Macedonia and Asia. *Rome to Philippi, and to Colossae via Ephesus; 63 A.D.*

Note: **Paul's Visit to Macedonia and Asia**—This visit is assumed from intentions indicated by Paul in his captivity epistles. It is obvious that Paul was confident that he would be released (Philip. 1:25-26; 2:17-18, 24; Philem. 22). To the Church at Philippi he made reference to his "coming to you again (Philip. 1:26) and wrote that "I trust in the Lord that I also myself shall come shortly" (Philip. 2:24). And to his friend Philemon in Colossae he made the request to "withal prepare me also a lodging: for I trust that through your prayers I shall be given to you" (Philem. 22). It is assumed that following his release from imprisonment in Rome he made the journey which he anticipated.

271. The epistle to the Hebrews was written. *Between 63 and 68 A.D.*

Note: **Authorship of the Epistle to the Hebrews**—The question "who wrote the epistle to the Hebrews?" has been a difficult one since ancient times. Today, Catholic scholarship holds that Paul was the author of the epistle, while Protestant scholars generally believe that he was not the epistle's author. The earliest Christian reference to the epistle was made by Clement of Alexandria (155-220 A.D.), and was quoted by

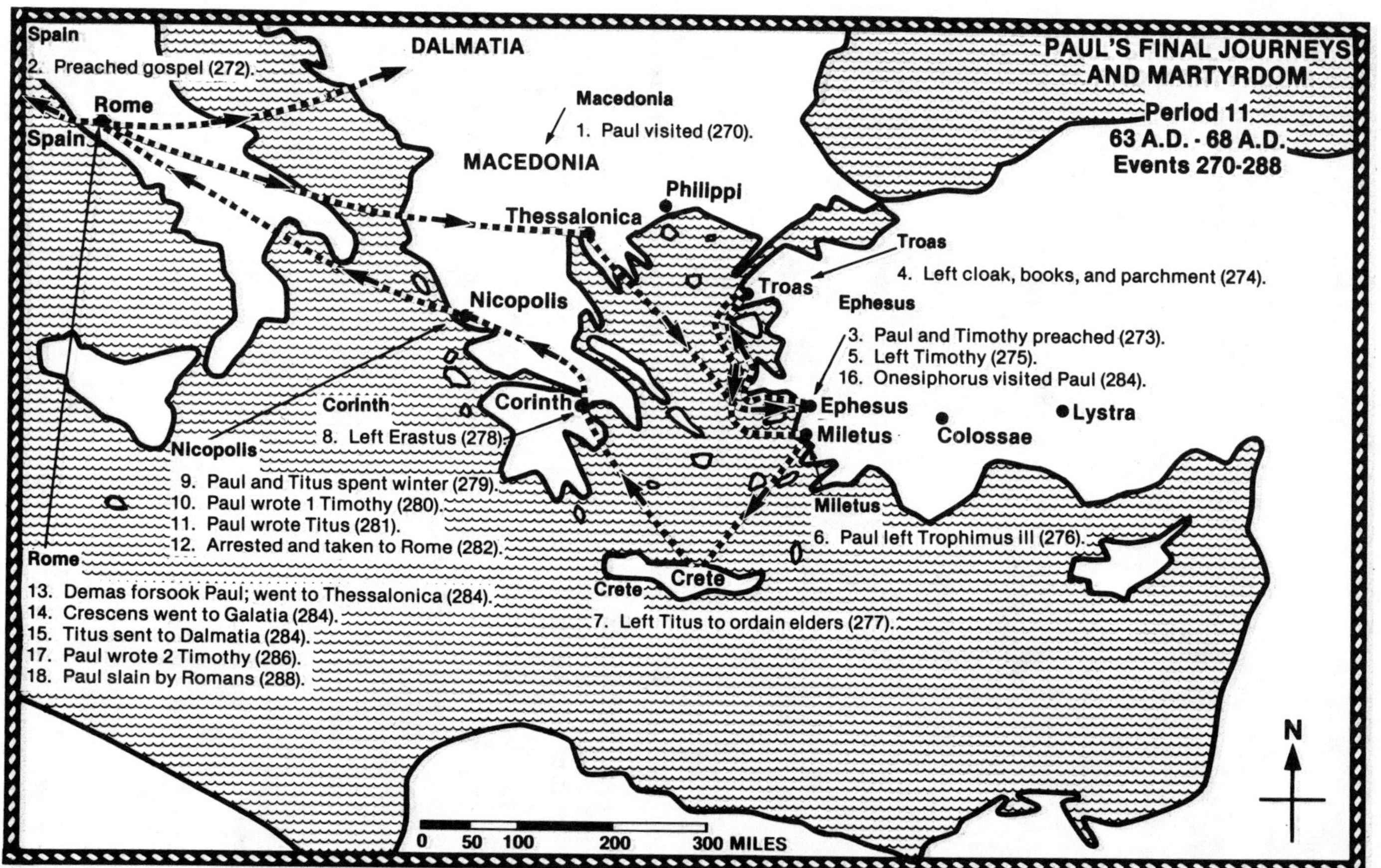
PAUL'S FINAL JOURNEYS AND MARTYRDOM
Period 11
63 A.D. - 68 A.D.
Events 270-288
Spain
2. Preached gospel (272).
DALMATIA
Rome
Spain
Macedonia
1. Paul visited (270).
MACEDONIA
Philippi
Thessalonica
Troas
4. Left cloak, books, and parchment (274).
Troas
Ephesus
3. Paul and Timothy preached (273).
5. Left Timothy (275).
16. Onesiphorus visited Paul (284).
Nicopolis
Corinth
Corinth
8. Left Erastus (278).
Ephesus
Lystra
Miletus
Colossae
Nicopolis
9. Paul and Titus spent winter (279).
10. Paul wrote 1 Timothy (280).
11. Paul wrote Titus (281).
12. Arrested and taken to Rome (282).
Miletus
6. Paul left Trophimus ill (276).
Rome
Crete
Crete
13. Demas forsook Paul; went to Thessalonica (284).
14. Crescens went to Galatia (284).
15. Titus sent to Dalmatia (284).
17. Paul wrote 2 Timothy (286).
18. Paul slain by Romans (288).
7. Left Titus to ordain elders (277).
N
0 50 100 200 300 MILES

the church historian Eusebius (*Historia Ecclesiae* VI, 14). Clement wrote that "The epistle is Paul's and that it was written to Hebrews in the Hebrew language, and that Luke translated it with zealous care and published it to the Greeks; whence it is that the same complexion of style is found in the translation of this Epistle and in the Acts." Origen (186-253 A.D.) expressed his understanding that the thoughts are Paul's thoughts, but that the "language and the composition that of one who recalled from memory and, as it were, made notes of what was said by his master" (*Historia Ecclesiae* VI, 25). Among the Catholics, the early eastern church accepted Paul as the author, but the western church did not accept his authorship until about the fourth century. Centuries later, at the time of the Protestant Reformation, Protestant scholars generally rejected the Pauline authorship of the epistle.

272. Paul journeyed to Spain and preached the gospel there. *64-66 A.D.*

Note: **Paul's Journey to Spain**—In his epistle to the Romans, Paul indicated his desire to "take my journey into Spain," and wrote that "I will come by you into Spain" (Rom. 15:24-28). Early Christian leaders wrote of his eventually traveling there. Clement of Rome (96 A.D.) alluded to Paul's "having come to the boundary of the West" (5:5-7). Mention of his trip to Spain is also found in the Muratorian Fragment, 170 A.D., and is mentioned by Athanasius, Epiphanius, Jerome, Theodoret, Chrysostom and St. Gregory. The Gnostic *Acts of Peter* relates in detail Paul's preparations for his journey into Spain also.

273. Paul returned to Ephesus, and taught there with Timothy. *Ephesus; 66 A.D.*

Note: **Paul's Preaching in the Ephesus Area**—Paul was there with Timothy (1 Tim. 1:3), and found that false teachers were teaching corrupt doctrines which mingled Oriental speculation, Greek philosophy and Jewish superstitions with the gospel. These teachers included Hymenaeus and Alexander, whom Paul "delivered unto Satan, that they may learn not to blaspheme" (1 Tim. 1:19-20), Philetus (2 Tim. 2:16-18), and Alexander the coppersmith, whom Paul wrote "did me much evil" and said, "The Lord reward him according to his works" (2 Tim. 4:14). He indicated that Alexander had withstood both his words and Timothy's (2 Tim. 4:15). Onesiphorous was very helpful to him while he was at Ephesus, and ministered to Paul in many ways (2 Tim. 1:18). It is likely that he made his headquarters at Ephesus, but took time to visit Colossae, Laodicea, Hierapolis, and the other congregations in Asia.

274. Paul visited Troas, and left his cloak, books and parchments there (2 Tim. 4:13). *Troas; 66 A.D.*

275. Paul left Timothy at Ephesus and went to Macedonia (1 Tim. 1:3). *Ephesus to Nicopolis, via Miletus, Crete(?), and Corinth; summer; 66 A.D.*

276. Paul left Trophimus at Miletus, because he suddenly became ill (2 Tim. 4:20). *Miletus, en route to Nicopolis; summer, 66 A.D.*

277. Paul went to Crete with Titus, and left him there to ordain elders in every city (Titus 1:5). *Crete; summer, 66 A.D.*

Note: **Paul's Visit to Crete**—Again, the only evidence of Paul's visit to Crete is found in the single verse cited above. It is not known if the trip to Crete was made during Paul's journey to Nicopolis or at another time.

278. Paul left Erastus at Corinth. *Corinth; summer, 66 A.D.*

Note: **Erastus**—All that is known of this individual is the allusion in Romans

16:23, which indicates he was "chamberlain of the city," or city treasurer—presumably of Corinth.

279. Titus spent the winter in Nicopolis (Titus 3:12). *Nicopolis; winter, 66-67 A.D.*

Note: **Nicopolis**—This city of Macedonia, located on the western shore of Macedonia about 130 miles northwest of Corinth, was situated on the Gulf of Actium on the Adriatic Sea. It was situated in the Roman province of Epirus, and was founded by Augustus in 31 B.C. on the site where his camp was located before the Battle of Actium. The city was a Roman colony, and was sustained by its commerce and fisheries. Paul apparently intended to open the missionary work on the western shores of Macedonia during his stay there. He had Artemas and Tychicus with him, and sent one or the other to Crete to relieve Titus so he could join him at Nicopolis (Titus 3:12). He requested that Titus bring Apollos and Zenas the lawyer with him when he came (Titus 3:13).

280. Paul wrote his first epistle to Timothy (1 Tim.) *Macedonia (Nicopolis?); 67 A.D.*

Note: **The Pastoral Epistles**—Three epistles are called the "Pastoral Epistles" because they were written to Paul's younger missionary companions, Timothy and Titus, instructing them concerning their duties as Church leaders in the congregations at Ephesus and Crete. These epistles, 1 Timothy, 2 Timothy, and Titus, constitute the fourth group of Paul's epistles, and were all written within the last two years of Paul's life. They are very similar in thought, phraseology, and style.

Note: **Paul's Intention to Rejoin Timothy at Ephesus**—In 1 Timothy 3:14-15 Paul indicated his intention to Timothy that he was "hoping to come unto thee shortly," but also indicated the possibility that he might "tarry long." It appears that Paul was never able to rejoin Timothy at Ephesus because of his arrest and imprisonment in Rome.

281. Paul wrote his epistle to Titus. *Nicopolis(?), 67 A.D.*

282. Paul was arrested and taken to Rome. *Nicopolis(?) to Rome; 67 A.D.*

Note: **The Neronian Persecution**—On July 19, 64 A.D., a fire broke out in Rome which raged for nine days and left much of the city in ashes. The Roman populace suspected that Nero was responsible for the fire, and clamored for retribution. Nero used the Christians as scapegoats, and blamed the destruction on them. Many Christians were arrested and put to death in a variety of cruel ways. This persecution changed the Roman perception of the Christians throughout the empire, and led to their persecution. It is not known why Paul was arrested and imprisoned, but Christians came to be regarded as enemies of the state, and it may well be that he was charged with sedition because of his prominence in the Christian world.

Note: **Nero**—When Paul appealed to Caesar (Acts 25:11), that Caesar was Nero. Lucius Domitius Ahenobarbus was born December 15, 37 A.D. His mother was a daughter of the nephew of the Emperor Tiberius, and she married the Emperor Claudius in 48 A.D. The emperor adopted Lucius in 50 A.D. and gave him new names, including the name Nero. He became the Roman Emperor in 54 A.D., when Claudius was murdered. For the first five years of his rule he was tutored by Burrus, a soldier, and the philosopher Seneca; they restrained him and kept his evil qualities in check. When he came of age, however, he threw off their restraints and engaged in excesses which were the scandal of Rome, and many believed him to be mad. A conspiracy against his life failed in 65 A.D., and he instituted a reign of terror against the Roman aristocracy and intellectual community, as well as against the Christians. Tradition holds that he had both Paul and Peter put to death. He was finally overthrown and committed suicide in 68 A.D.

283. Paul was treated as an "evil doer" and was kept in bonds and chains (2 Tim. 2:9; 1:16). *Rome; 67-68 A.D.*

284. Most of Paul's friends deserted him, or were sent away (2 Tim. 4:10-11). *Rome; 67-68 A.D.*

***Note:* Paul's Companions in Rome**—Paul indicated that Demas had forsaken him and had gone to Thessalonica; Crescens was gone to Galatia; and Titus was sent unto Dalmatia. Luke was with him. (2 Tim. 4:10-11.) Onesiphorus came from Ephesus and diligently sought Paul out. He often refreshed Paul. Eubulus, Pudens, Linus and Claudia also visited him (2 Tim. 4:21). The apostle wrote and asked Timothy to join him and to bring John Mark (2 Tim. 4:11), as well as the personal items he had accidently left at Troas (2 Tim. 4:13). He asked Timothy to be sure to come before winter (2 Tim. 4:21).

285. In Paul's first hearing before the Romans he stood alone (2 Tim. 4:16-17).

***Note:* Paul's First Defense**—Paul wrote that "the Lord stood with me, and strengthened me" and that he "was delivered out of the mouth of the lion" (2 Tim. 4:16-17).

286. Paul wrote his second epistle to Timothy. *Rome; 67 A.D.*

287. Paul's summation of his life's work: "I have fought a good fight, I have finished my course, I have kept the faith: Henceforth there is laid up for me a crown of righteousness, which the Lord, the righteous judge, shall give me at that day . . ." **(2 Tim. 4:7-8).**

288. Paul was slain by the Romans. *Outside Rome; 68 A.D.*

***Note:* Paul's Martyrdom**—Roman law provided that a period of ten days had to pass between the time a criminal was convicted and the time he was executed, so that a pardon might be granted by the emperor if he chose to do so. Roman custom was to take an individual outside of the city to execute him, especially if his death might cause a demonstration by the population of the city. Roman citizens were usually beheaded with a sword, which saved Paul the usual Christian death of being crucified or being smeared with pitch and then being set on fire. According to St. Jerome, Paul was martyred in the fourteenth year of Nero's reign (between October 13, 67 A.D. and June 9, 68 A.D.). Tradition holds that he was executed on the Ostian Way, about two miles southwest of the city.

Period 12

PETER'S LATER MINISTRY AND MARTYRDOM; THE WRITING OF THE SYNOPTIC GOSPELS

61 A.D. to 68 A.D.

Matthew, Mark, Luke, Acts, 1Peter, Jude, 2Peter

Peter's Ministry in Asia Minor
Peter Comes to Rome
Mark, Luke, and Matthew Are Written
The Acts of the Apostles Are Written
First Peter Is Written and Delivered by Silas to Asia Minor
The Epistle of Jude Is Written
Second Peter Is Written
Peter Is Martyred by the Romans

289. Peter preached outside of Palestine. *Syria and Asia Minor(?); 44-61 A.D.(?).*

***Note:* Peter's Mission in Asia Minor**—Little is known of Peter's ministry after his miraculous escape from imprisonment in Jerusalem at the hands of Herod Agrippa I. The scriptural record indicates only that he "departed, and went into another place" (Acts 12:17, 44 A.D.). It is known that he visited the Church at Antioch (see #120, 49 A.D.), and that he attended the Council at Jerusalem (see #126, 49 A.D.). After these events, the book of Acts gives no further information concerning his travels. Bible scholars generally portray him as becoming a minister to the Jews of the Dispersion. It is asserted that he preached in Syria, and had Antioch as his base for a period of time. It is inferred from his first epistle that he also labored in northern Asia Minor because he wrote to the Church members "scattered throughout Pontus, Galatia, Cappadocia, Asia and Bithynia" (1 Pet. 1:1). The instruction given to Paul during his second missionary journey not to go into Bithynia (#138, 49 A.D.) is taken by some as an indication that Peter was laboring in that area during that period.

290. Peter probably visited Corinth (1 Cor. 1:12; 3:22). *Corinth; before 56 A.D.*

***Note:* Peter's Visit to Corinth**—This visit is assumed by Paul's indication, in 1 Corinthians, that some of the members of Corinth were followers of Cephas (the Aramaic name which Christ gave to Simon when he called him to be a disciple (John 1:42). It means "a stone." The corresponding Greek name is "Petros." The length of his stay in Corinth is not known. Obviously, it took place before Paul wrote 1 Corinthians. Paul indicates that Peter was probably accompanied by his wife in his missionary travels (1 Cor. 9:5).

291. Peter came to Rome. *61 A.D.(?).*

***Note:* Peter and the Church in Rome**—There is little evidence to support the belief that Peter founded the Church in Rome, nor that he labored there for many years. There were Christians there before 50 A.D., assuming that Aquila and Priscilla were converted before being expelled from Rome and coming to Corinth (Acts 18:1-2). This was more than a decade before there is any record of Peter coming to that city. The large circle of members in Rome (Rom. 16) had been there "many years" (Rom. 15:23) before Paul wrote his epistle to them in 57 A.D. The New Testament never reports a visit by Peter to that city. Paul's epistle to the Romans gives no evidence that Peter is there nor that he established the Church in that city. The more general assumption is that Peter came to Rome late in his life, only a few years before his martyrdom. It is quite probable, however, that Paul was in Rome during a portion of the time of Paul's first imprisonment (60-63 A.D.). He may have remained past the time of Paul's martyrdom (c. 68 A.D.) until he, himself, was martyred. Both men were probably associated with the Church there, and probably were jointly involved in efforts to preserve the history of Christ's ministry as they guided the efforts of Luke in writing their gospels. A study of Peter's epistles indicates that he was well acquainted with Paul's epistles to the Romans and to the Ephesians, an indication that he held Paul in high esteem and worked directly with him.

292. Peter's companions in Rome were Mark and Silas (Silvanus) (1 Pet. 5:12-13). *Rome; between 61 and 68 A.D.*

293. Mark wrote the gospel of Mark. *Rome; between 61 and 70 A.D.*

***Note:* The Synoptic Gospels**—Matthew, Mark and Luke are called the "Synoptic Gospels" because they "see the whole together" and present similar views of the teachings, travels and ministry of Jesus Christ. The authors of the three gospels were apparently aware of each other's gospels, and it is evident that none of the three was written independently of the others. Each author describes the Savior's life from his own point of view, in a manner which accomplishes his own purposes. *Matthew* wrote for the Jews, and sought to portray Jesus as the Messiah. He showed that Jesus' life fulfilled the many prophecies of the Christ found in the law and the prophets. He emphasized Jesus' authority, his tenderness, and his role as King and Judge. *Mark* wrote for the Romans, and emphasized Christ's daily actions, his energy and humility, and the popular response to his ministry. *Luke*, who wrote for the Greeks, stressed Christ's humanitarian aspects—his love and sympathy for mankind, as he depicted him as the great High Priest and the Savior of all mankind. The gospel of *John* was written later, apparently as an effort to supplement the other three gospels with details which they had omitted. John wrote to stimulate belief in Jesus as the Only Begotten Son of God, and depicted his obedience to his Heavenly Father during his mortal ministry.

***Note:* Order of Writing of the Synoptic Gospels**—It is generally asserted that Mark was written before Luke and Matthew, and that the two latter authors had access to the gospel of Mark as they wrote. This conclusion is drawn because of the numerous parallels between Mark and the other two gospels.

***Note:* The Language of the Gospel of Mark**—Mark wrote in Greek, for the Romans. According to Papias (quoted by Eusebius in his *Ecclesiastical History* III.39), Mark was Peter's interpreter in Rome. It can be assumed that Mark drew heavily on Peter's personal reminiscences of the Savior, and that Peter either supervised the writing of the gospel or the gospel was written based on Mark's recollections of Peter's sermons and personal conversations with him. Mark also was closely associated with Paul in Rome during Paul's first Roman imprisonment, and probably gained many insights from him.

294. Luke wrote the gospel of Luke. *Rome; between 60 and 63 A.D.*

Note: **The Time of the Writing of Luke's Gospel**—Scholars place various dates on the writing of the third gospel—from 57 to 74 A.D. Most believe, however, that it was written (A) at Rome, during Paul's first imprisonment there (though Luke was also with Paul during his second Roman imprisonment, according to 2 Tim. 4:11); (B) after the gospel of Mark (because it makes use of that gospel); and (C) a year prior to the writing of the book of Acts (because it forms an introduction to that book). There is a good possibility that Luke and Mark were writing their gospels at the same time, and in the same city, under the direction of Peter and Paul.

295. Matthew wrote the gospel of Matthew. *Place unknown; between 61 and 70 A.D.*

Note: **The Gospel of Matthew**—It is frequently asserted by Bible scholars that this gospel was written in Hebrew or Aramaic for Jewish converts to Christianity in Palestine. It is clear that it was written after the gospel of Mark, for it is dependent upon that gospel. Scholars assert that the gospel actually was circulated in Greek, through a translation from Aramaic probably made by Matthew himself.

296. Luke wrote the Acts of the Apostles. *Rome; between 62 and 67 A.D.*

Note: **The Time of the Writing of Acts**—It is generally assumed that the book of Acts was written before the end of Paul's first imprisonment in Rome (prior to 63 A.D.) because of its abrupt ending, which fails to tell the outcome of Paul's imprisonment and gives no details of the last half decade or more of his life. Yet it appears that Acts was written after the gospel of Luke, and that gospel was written after the gospel of Mark. Various scholars tend to date the three books earlier or later, according to their personal views. In reality, there is little tangible evidence upon which to base any solid conclusions concerning their dating.

297. Peter wrote his first epistle to the Church in Asia Minor. *Rome; 64 A.D.*

Note: **Babylon a Symbol for Rome**—In 1 Peter 5:13 the epistle conveys greetings from "the church that is at Babylon." It appears that in this epistle, as in the Revelation of John (Rev. 14:8; 16:19; 17:5; 18:2, 10, 21), Babylon is cryptic allusion to Rome. This epistle was apparently written during the early stages of the intense persecution of the Christians, which occurred when the emperor Nero blamed the Christians for burning Rome in 64 A.D.

298. Peter's epistle was delivered to the churches in Asia Minor by Silas (1 Pet. 5:12). *Rome to Asia Minor; 64-65 A.D.*

299. Jude wrote his epistle to warn of heresy within the Church. *Jerusalem(?); 67 or 68 A.D.*

Note: **The Epistle of Jude**—The epistle indicates that it is written by "Jude, a servant of Jesus Christ and a brother of James." This is believed to be Judas who was the brother of the Lord Jesus Christ as well as the brother of James (Matt. 13:55; Mark 6:3; possibly 1 Cor. 9:5). It is not the apostle Judas referred to in Luke 6:16 and Acts 1:13, who was also known as Lebbaeus and Thaddaeus. Neither is it Judas Iscariot, referred to in John 14:22. This epistle is one of the "general" or "Catholic" epistles placed at the end of the New Testament. It possibly may have been directed, originally, to the Church at Syrian Antioch. Place and date of origin are uncertain, and were controversial even in earliest times. The epistle is closely related to 2 Peter, which also addresses the serious heresy which suddenly manifested itself. Some scholars date the epistle as late as the second century, and attribute it to an anonymous author.

300. Peter wrote his second epistle to the Church in Asia Minor. *Rome; 67 or 68 A.D.*

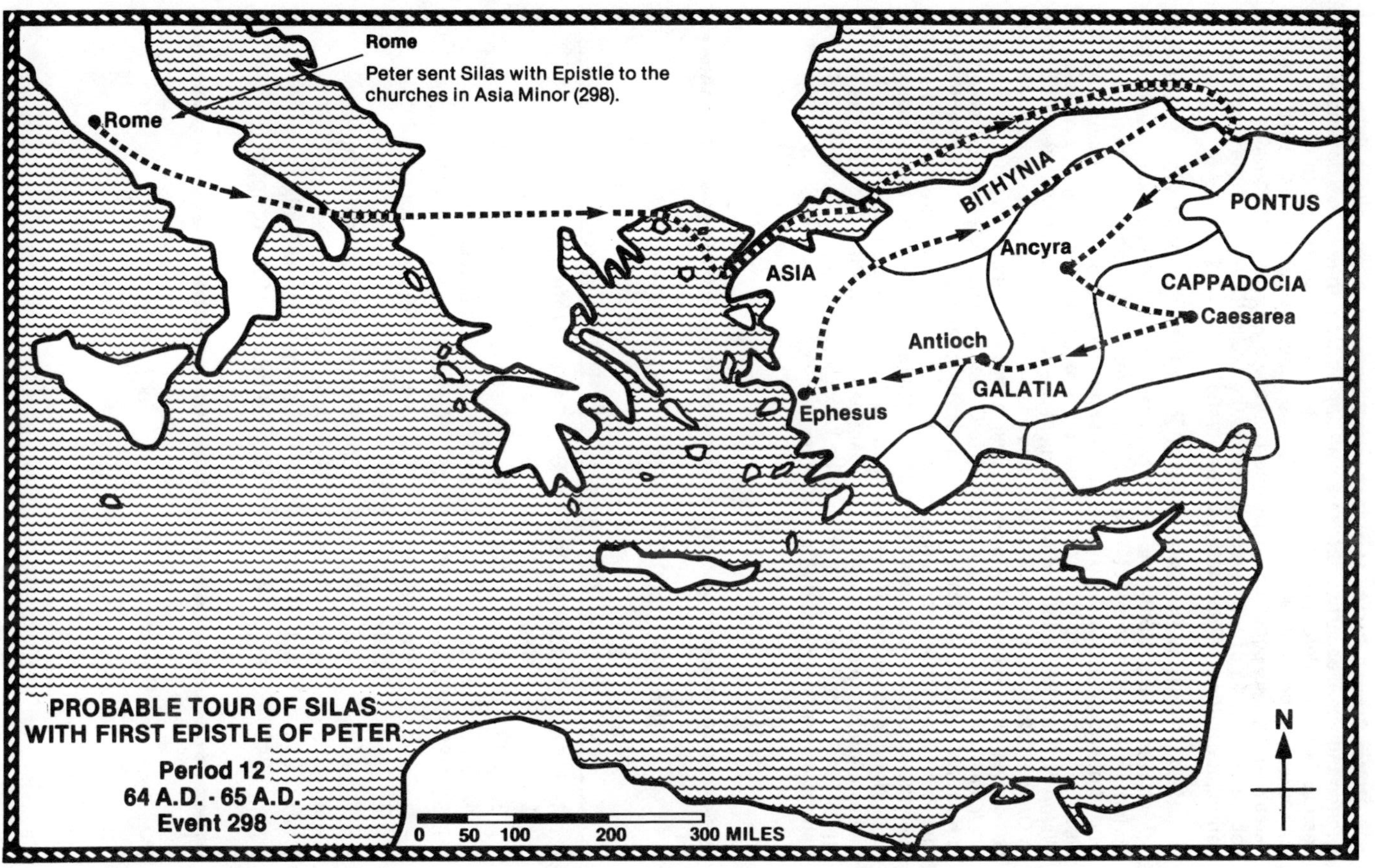

Rome
Peter sent Silas with Epistle to the
churches in Asia Minor (298).
Rome
BITHYNIA
PONTUS
ASIA
Ancyra
CAPPADOCIA
Caesarea
Antioch
GALATIA
Ephesus
PROBABLE TOUR OF SILAS
WITH FIRST EPISTLE OF PETER
Period 12
64 A.D. - 65 A.D.
Event 298
0
50
100
200
300 MILES
N

Note: **Second Peter**—Many scholars have pointed out various links between 2 Peter and Jude, asserting that one was copied from the other. The tendency has been to deny that Peter was the author of the epistle, ascribing it to an anonymous author writing between 90 and 110 A.D. Like Jude, the epistle deals with a serious heresy which had occurred within the Church. Speculation concerning the exact source and nature of the heresy furnishes the basis for many of the theories concerning the authorship and dating of the epistle.

301. Peter was slain by the Romans. *Outside Rome; 68 A.D.*

Note: **Peter's Martyrdom**—It is believed that Peter, like Paul, was martyred during the Neronian persecution of the Christians. Dionysius, the bishop of Corinth who wrote about 175 A.D., expressed his understanding that "they taught together also in Italy, and were martyred on the same occasion" (Eusebius, *Ecclesiastical History* II.25.8). The validity of his statement has not been fully accepted. According to Origen (c. 225 A.D.), Peter was crucified head-downward, at his own request, since he believed himself unworthy to be crucified in the same manner as his Lord (Eusebius, *Ecclesiastical History* III.1.2). According to Gaius of Rome, Peter was buried on what is now the Vatican Hill. The emperor Constantine built a church there on the belief that Peter was martyred or buried there. The exact location of Peter's burial site has been the object of historical and archaeological research and debate for many years.

Note: **Apocraphal Works Ascribed to Peter**—Various other works besides those canonized in the Bible have been ascribed to Peter. These include "The Preaching of Peter," the "Gospel of Peter," the "Apocalypse of Peter," and an "Epistle of Peter to James" connected with the Clementine Homilies.

MAJOR DISCOURSES IN THE BOOK OF ACTS

	Item No.	*Person*	*Scripture Reference*	*Description*
1.	12	Peter	Acts 2:14-36	Day of Pentecost
2.	17	Peter	Acts 3:12-26	Temple in Jerusalem
3.	39	Stephen	Acts 7:1-54	Defense Before Sanhedrin
4.	76	Peter	Acts 10:24-43	Cornelius and Company
5.	78	Peter	Acts 11:1-18	Circumcised Church Members
6.	106	Paul	Acts 13:14-41	Synagogue at Antioch
7.	154	Paul	Acts 17:16-33	Mars' Hill
8.	213	Paul	Acts 20:18-38	Farewell to Ephesian Church
9.	226	Paul	Acts 22:1-21	Account of Conversion
10.	235	Paul	Acts 24:10-21	Defense Before Felix
11.	242	Paul	Acts 26:1-29	Defense Before Agrippa

Period 13

THE CHRISTIAN EXODUS FROM PALESTINE AND THE FALL OF JERUSALEM

62 A.D. to 73 A.D.

A Jewish Court Executes James and Other Christians
Symeon Becomes Leader of the Christians in Jerusalem
Most of the Christians Flee Palestine to Pella or to Asia Minor
The Unjust Rule of Procurator Florus Causes Unrest in Jerusalem
Florus Raids the Temple Treasury and Crucifies Leading Citizens
The Jews Discontinue the Daily Sacrifice for the Roman Emperor
Jewish Insurgents Seize the Antonia Fortress
Zealots Capture Masada and Part of Jerusalem
Roman Troops from Syria Are Defeated at Beth-horon Pass
Vespasian Leads the Roman Army Into Palestine
Josephus Becomes an Interpreter for the Romans
Roman Attacks Are Suspended Because of Nero's Suicide
Three Jewish Rivals Struggle for Power in Jerusalem
Vespasian Again Attacks and Conquers All of Palestine Except Jerusalem and Three Forts
Vespasian Leaves for Rome to Become the Emperor
Titus, Vespasian's Son, Conquers Jerusalem After a Five-Month Seige
Masada Falls After a Mass Suicide by the Zealots
Yohanan Establishes a School of Rabbinical Study at Jamnia
A New Sanhedrin Is Established at Jamnia

302. Porcius Festus, the Roman Procurator of Judaea, suddenly died. *Caesarea; 62 A.D.*

303. The Jewish high priest, Ananus, convened a council of judges. They illegally condemned Jesus' brother James, and other Christians, to death. *Jerusalem; 62 A.D.*

***Note:* Jewish Courts Not Empowered to Enact Capital Punishment**—The Jewish leaders, obviously attempting to suppress the Christians by taking illegal actions in the absence of Roman rule, condemned James and the other Christians to death by stoning. The Romans had allowed the Jewish courts to govern in domestic matters, but the Jews were expressly prohibited from enacting the death penalty.

Note: **Ananus**—Ananus, son of Ananus, was a Sadducee. This execution was one of his first acts as high priest. He was able to carry out the executions because the newly appointed Roman Procurator, Albinus, had not yet arrived in Palestine. His period of office was only three months because Herod Agrippa II had him removed due to his illegal act.

304. Herod Agrippa II removed Ananus from power to prevent Roman punishment of the Jews. *Jerusalem; 62 A.D.*

305. Symeon, the son of Clopas, became leader of the Christians in Jerusalem. *Jerusalem; 62 A.D.*

Note: **Symeon**—Eusebius, in his *Ecclesiastical History* III.11, quotes a statement by Hegesippus, who indicates that Clopas was a brother to Joseph, the husband of Mary the mother of Jesus.

306. The Jerusalem Christians received a revelation telling them to flee from Jerusalem because the city was doomed. Many of them settled in Pella, one of the cities of the Decapolis, east of the Jordan River. *Jerusalem to Pella; between 62 and 66 A.D.*

Note: **The "Oracle"**—Eusebius (*Ecclesiastical History* III.5.3) records that this "oracle," or revelation, was given to those in Jerusalem who were "approved," and it gave specific instructions to flee to the city of Pella. This warning enabled the Jerusalem Christians to escape the Roman attacks and seige of Jerusalem. From that time on, Pella became an important center of the Church.

307. Many other Christians from Palestine migrated to Asia Minor. *Palestine to Asia; 62-66 A.D.*

Note: **The Christian Migration From Palestine**—This migration caused by prophecies foretelling the fall of Jerusalem and by the rapidly deteriorating political affairs throughout Palestine served to remove most of the Christian leadership from the Jerusalem area. The apostle John apparently moved to Ephesus. Philip and his daughters (Acts 21:8-9) moved from Caesarea and made their home in Hierapolis, in Phrygia. It appears that many Christians still remained in Palestine, however, particularly in Galilee and in the coastal areas. The tumultuous political events which were beginning to take place in Palestine left little doubt that war with Rome was not far distant. Serious provocations of the Jews in Caesarea, a Gentile city, had caused considerable unrest during Felix' rule, and the Jewish population there had lost many of their civil rights. Unrest in Caesarea between the Jews and the Greeks, who continually sought to annoy and insult the Jews there, was a significant cause of the rebellion which occurred in 66 A.D.

308. Clodius Albinus became the Roman Procurator. *Caesarea; 62-64 A.D.*

309. Gessius Florus replaced Albinus as the Roman Procurator. *Caesarea; 64-66 A.D.*

310. The Romans, led by Florus, raided the temple treasury and seized seventeen talents, claiming they were required for the emperor's service. The Jews, deeming this an act of sacrilege, rioted. In retaliation, Florus seized a number of leading citizens and crucified them, then sent the Roman troops to plunder a portion of Jerusalem as punishment for the riot. *Jerusalem; spring, 66 A.D.*

Note: **Florus' Greed and Unjust Rule**—Florus' lust for wealth and power caused him to institute policies which embraced extortion, bribery and unjustly severe punishments for the Jews. It was his unjust and brutal conduct that caused escalation of the Zealot resistance movement against the Romans, and paved the way for the Jewish revolt.

311. The Jews destroyed the passages between the Antonia Fortress and the outer court of the temple so the Roman soldiers couldn't seize the temple area. *Jerusalem temple; spring, 66 A.D.*

312. Cestius Gallus, Roman Procurator of Syria, and Herod Agrippa II, sent Neapolitanus, a military tribune, from Antioch to investigate the troubles at Jerusalem. He conveyed Agrippa's exhortation to pay the arrears of tribute and restore the broken colonnades connecting the temple with the fortress. The people shouted him down and drove him from the city. *Jerusalem; spring, 66 A.D.*

313. Eleazar, captain of the temple, persuaded the priests to discontinue offering the daily sacrifice for the welfare of the Roman emperor.

Note: **Cessation of the Daily Sacrifice an Open Act of Revolution**—This act was interpreted by both sides as an open act of revolt against the Romans. Many responsible citizens took desperate measures to reverse the revolutionary trend, but failed.

314. Jewish insurgents seized the Antonia Fortress and wiped out the Roman garrison. *Jerusalem; September, 66 A.D.*

315. Jewish Zealots captured Masada, the Roman fort west of the Dead Sea. *Masada; fall, 66 A.D.*

316. Menahem led a force of Zealots to Jerusalem and occupied the western portion of the city. Eleazar, captain of the temple, did not want a rival leader, so the two factions fought for several days. Menahem and some of his leaders were captured and killed. The remaining Zealots fled back to Masada. *Jerusalem; fall, 66 A.D.*

317. Josephus warned the Jews of their foolishness in resisting Rome, but became a leader of the Jewish forces in Galilee. *66 A.D.*

Note: **Josephus**—Flavius Josephus (Jewish name: Joseph ben Matathias) was born 37 or 38 A.D., and died sometime after 100 A.D. He was from a priestly family and a descendant of the Hasmoneans. At 16 he lived for three years in the wilderness as a student of the hermit, Bannus. While still a youth he joined the Pharisees. In 64 A.D. he journeyed to Rome to plead for the liberation of some priests whom the procurator Felix had sent to be tried by Nero. He was greatly impressed by the splendor and might of Rome which he observed during his journey. When he returned to Palestine, he found his country engaged in a revolt against Rome. He reluctantly joined the fight, and became a leader of the revolutionary forces in the Galilee area. When his forces fell to Vespasian's army after a 47-day seige of the town of Jotapata, he was brought before Vespasian as a prisoner. On that occasion he predicted to Vespasian that he, Vespasian, would soon become the emperor of Rome. When his prediction was fulfilled in 69 A.D., Vespasian made him a free man, and had him serve during the Jewish war as an interpreter and mediator. After the war he went to Rome and settled there with the rights of a Roman citizen with a

Roman pension. From the time of his surrender to the end of his life he remained a client of the Flavian emperors, so he adopted the name Flavius. In Rome he undertook a literary career. His first work was the *Wars of the Jews*, which told the story of the Jewish revolt against Rome. Twenty years later (c. 93-94 A.D.) he wrote his *Antiquities of the Jews*, a history of the Jews in twenty books. He attached his life story as an appendix. Then he wrote an eloquent apology for Judaism in two books, *Against Apion.*

318. Cestius Gallus marched his legionary troops south from Syria. He occupied the northern portion of Jerusalem, but withdrew when he determined his troops were insufficient to control the city. His troops were ambushed in the Pass of Beth-horon and defeated. *Syria to Jerusalem to Beth-horon Pass; November, 66 A.D.*

***Note:* Jewish National Mobilization**—This site was the same place where Judas Maccabaeus had won several victories and suffered severe losses during the Maccabean Wars over a century earlier. This victory served to discredit the Jewish moderates who were still seeking peace. The insurgents used the victory to mobilize the entire Jewish population in preparation for a war of liberation.

319. Vespasian led the Roman army into Palestine the following spring. He captured Galilee, Peraea, western Judaea and Idumaea, and prepared to lay seige on Jerusalem. *Syria to Jerusalem; spring, 67 A.D.*

***Note:* Vespasian**—Titus Flavius Vespasianus was the Roman emperor from 69 to 79 A.D., and founded the Flavian Dynasty. He was born to a prosperous Italian family on November 17, 9 A.D. He rose to power in the Roman army, serving as a Praetor during Caligula's reign, a legion commander under Claudius. He became a Consul Suffectus in 51 A.D.; twelve years later he was proconsul of Africa, and accompanied Nero to Greece in 66 A.D. He was given command of three legions to suppress the Jewish revolt. He left Palestine to become emperor, arriving at Rome in September, 70 A.D. When his son Titus conquered Jerusalem, he joined his father in Rome and Vespasian made him a high official in the Roman government. Vespasian's administration was effective, and he saved the empire when it was in danger of collapse. He died on June 24, 79 A.D., and his son Titus succeeded him as emperor.

320. Yohanan ben Zakkai, a rabbi, was smuggled out of Jerusalem and brought before Vespasian. He hailed Vespasian as the future emperor and prophesied that he would conquer Jerusalem, which won him favor in Vespasian's eyes. *Outside Jerusalem; 69 A.D.(?).*

***Note:* Yohanan ben Zakkai**—This man was a leading rabbi from the school of Hillel. He became the stabilizing force for the Jews after the Roman war.

321. The Roman Emperor Nero committed suicide when revolt broke out in Gaul, Spain and Africa. *Rome; June 9, 68 A.D.*

322. Rivals at Rome attempted to claim Nero's throne. Vespasian suspended his attack for a year, waiting to determine the results of the power struggle. *Rome and Palestine; 68-69 A.D.*

***Note:* Nero's Successors**—A year of anarchy followed Nero's death. Three men came to power in rapid succession but were unable to maintain stability in the government. These men were Galba, a governor in Spain; Otho, a previous husband of Poppea and a friend of Nero's; and Vitellius, a general in Spain. It was Galba's revolt which caused Nero's suicide; Galba was murdered by Otho; and he in turn was vanquished by Vitellius and his garrisons from Germany.

323. Three rival leaders of Jewish factions established themselves in Jerusalem during Vespasian's inactivity: Simon bar Giora (the city suburbs), John of Gischala (the outer Temple court), and Eleazar, son of Simon (the inner Temple courts). *Jerusalem; 68-69 A.D.*

324. Vespasian again attacked. He conquered all of Palestine except Jerusalem and three forts: Herodian, Masada, and Machaerus. *Palestine, June, 69 A.D.*

325. Vespasian was proclaimed emperor of Rome by the Roman commanders and armies of the eastern provinces. His partisans seized Rome on his behalf. *July, 69 A.D.*

326. Vespasian left Palestine to assume control of the empire at Rome. He summoned Titus, his eldest son, from Alexandria to complete the suppression of the Jewish revolt. *Palestine; fall, 69 A.D.*

327. Titus began the seige of Jerusalem in April, 70 A.D. The city fell in five months. *Jerusalem; April-September, 70 A.D.*

***Note:* The Seige of Jerusalem**—The combined armies in Jerusalem numbered about 25,000 men; the Romans had four legions and many auxiliary units, totaling about 80,000 men. Titus began his attack and seige in April; by the end of August the temple had fallen, and before the end of September all resistance in Jerusalem had ended. The main Roman camp was set up on the west of the city, with a secondary camp on the Mount of Olives. The third wall was breached from the west, the second wall from the north. The Romans moved their headquarters to the "Assyrian Camp" within the third wall, and from there launched their attack against the Herodian towers and the Fortress of Antonia. The defenders repelled them and destroyed many of the Roman seige engines. Titus then decided to starve out the city, and built a seige wall around it. When he renewed his attack in July, Titus was able to storm the Antonia Fortress and overrun the temple sanctuary. The temple was burned on the ninth of the Hebrew month of Ab, and that has been a day of mourning for all Jewry ever since. The Romans conquered the whole lower city, but the upper city held out until the eighth of Elul, a month later. The destruction of the city culminated a prolonged attack and seige of 143 days. More than 600,000 Jews were slain, and many thousands more were led into captivity. The city was left desolate, but people were allowed to reenter the city and settle there. Jerusalem really held no significance as a city for another sixty years.

328. Herodian, Machaerus and Masada fell to the Romans. *70-73 A.D.*

***Note:* The Fall of Masada**—The Zealots at Masada held out until April or May, 73 A.D. They watched as the Romans forced Jewish slaves to build a huge ramp up to the high plateau on which the fortress was located. When they saw that no hope for escape remained, they decided to commit mass suicide rather than fall into the hands of their Roman conquerers.

329. Yohanan ben Zakkai received permission from the Romans to set up a school of rabbinical study at Jamnia. *Jamnia, in western Judaea; between 70 and 80 A.D.*

***Note:* The Rabbinical School at Jamnia**—Since Yohanan and his colleagues all belonged to the school of Hillel, there was greater agreement on matters of interpretation than previously, when the school of Shammai held opposing viewpoints. This school labored for over a century on the codification of Jewish laws called the Mishna, which previously had been transmitted orally. The collection of laws is specifically attributed to Rabbi Judah the Prince (born 135 A.D.). The Mishna is divided into six orders, which in turn are grouped into sixty-three treatises. These treatises embraced the entire Jewish religious and legal system which had been taught in the schools of Palestine up to that time.

330. A new Jewish Sanhedrin was established at Jamnia. *Jamnia; between 70 and 80 A.D.*

Note: **The New Sanhedrin**—The Sanhedrin formed at Jamnia differed greatly from the previous Sanhedrin which functioned at Jerusalem. The earlier body was comprised of the chief priests and elders, with the current high priest functioning as its president. It was recognized by the Romans as the national administration for Palestine. The new Sanhedrin lacked the power and authority of its predecessor. It was made up of doctors of the law, and functioned mainly as a supreme court for the establishing and codifying of Jewish law. After a while it acquired limited recognition in the eyes of Rome, and served to a limited degree as the body which rebuilt Israel's shattered national life.

331. Palestine was governed by Roman military rulers rather than civil rulers. It became an imperial province of Rome, and was governed by a legate with legionary forces at his command. *Palestine; 67 to 135 A.D.*

Note: **The Beginning of Military Rule in Palestine**—Military rule began with the appointment of Vespasian to suppress the Jewish revolt in 67 A.D. Roman legates were considered official emissaries of the emperor rather than local governors.

Period 14

THE LATER MINISTRY OF JOHN; THE "JOHANNINE" WRITINGS

60 A.D. to 100 A.D.

John, 1 John, 2 John, 3 John, Revelation

John's Ministry in Asia Minor
John Writes the Gospel of John
Gnostic Heresies Spread and Influence the Church
John Writes 1 John, 2 John, and 3 John
John Is Banished to the Isle of Patmos
John Writes Revelation
John Is Released When Nerva Becomes Emperor
John Dies or Is Translated

332. John moved to Ephesus. *Palestine to Ephesus(?); 66 A.D.(?).*

***Note:* Tradition Concerning John's Residence in Ephesus**—The dominant tradition of the early Church concerning the apostle John is that he moved to Ephesus after years of leadership in Jerusalem. The main source for this tradition is Irenaeus, who claimed that while he was "still a boy" (Eusebius, *Ecclesiastical History* V.20.5) he heard detailed reports directly from Polycarp of John's presence and work in Ephesus; reports of John's activities there also came from Papias (*Her.* III.3.4; V.33.4). Reports from others also relate specific incidences of John's activities there: Apollonius tells of John's raising a dead man at Ephesus; Clement of Alexandria tells how John converted a robber to Christ; Iranaeus tells how John opposed the heretic Cerinthus, and how John, in his old age, was carried to meetings at Ephesus where he repeatedly taught, "Little children, love one another."

333. John wrote the gospel of John. *Ephesus; 80 A.D.(?).*

***Note:* Dating the Writings of John**—There is no solid evidence upon which to base the dating of any of the five Johannine writings. Scholarly estimates of dates, particularly of the gospel of John, range from as early as 40 A.D. to as late as 110 A.D. The *Muratorian Fragment* (II.9-23) states that John was with the rest of the apostles when he was led to write his gospel. If this is true, it would suggest an early date, while the other apostles were still alive, and would probably place the location of the writing of the fourth gospel in Palestine rather than Asia Minor. The *Muratorian Fragment* (c. 180 A.D.) also asserts that John wrote his gospel in obedience to a special revelation given to him and to Andrew. There is no solid evidence to date the writing of the three epistles of John, and it is not known if they were written before or after the book of Revelation. They were written to combat heresies that were arising in the Church. These heresies are usually assumed by scholars to be Gnosticism, but this assumption does not afford any chronologically definitive clue. John states in Revelation that he received his visions while on the isle of Patmos (Rev. 1:9); yet the length of his stay on that island is unknown except for a statement in Eusebius' history (III.18, 20) that "the apostle and evangelist John" was banished to Patmos, and that on the accession of Nerva (96 A.D.) he returned from the island and took up his abode in Ephesus. It is often assumed that John was banished during the persecutions instigated by the Roman emperor Domitian, who ruled from 81 to 96, but no significant direct evidence sustains this assumption.

334. John wrote his first epistle. *Ephesus(?).*

Note: **The Gnostic Heresies**—John wrote to combat heresies which were creeping into the early Church. It is thought that these heresies were arising among the Gnostics, though that assumption is not certain. It may still have been the influence of the Judaizers which was leading the early members astray. The term *Gnosticism* is a modern term used to classify a variety of religious sects that existed from the first through the ninth centuries. Gnosticism was a philosophy which promised salvation by knowledge. The Gnostics believed that God was too holy to have created the material world with all its baseness and corruption. They believed that the universe was made and controlled by hostile powers, or "emanations." From the supreme diety there had been a series of "emanations," each somewhat inferior to its predecessor; the last of these emanations, or "aeons," created this world. They held that matter is evil, while spirit is good, and that salvation was attained by escaping from the realm of matter into the realm of the spirit. They challenged the Christian teaching that the Son of God came to earth and took up a human body; they asked how a pure spirit could have anything to do with a material body—a body which their philosophy led them to regard as evil. Their solutions took two forms. *Docetism* held that Christ was not really human, but simply an illusion that appeared to be a man but had no real existence. *Cerinthianism* asserted that Christ's spirit did not actually inhabit his human body until after his baptism, and that it left him before his death on the cross. Both of these "solutions" would have negated the gospel of Jesus Christ completely if they had become the standard interpretation of Christianity. Several ethical conclusions were also drawn by the Gnostics which affected religious thought. One was asceticism, which held that since the body was matter it was evil and should be kept under strict control—all its appetites curbed and its impulses suppressed or disregarded. The opposite assumption was that since the body was unreal and temporary, its acts were inconsequential; full gratification of physical desires would have no ultimate effect on the salvation of the spirit, according to their philosophy, because only the spirit would survive.

335. John wrote his second epistle. *Ephesus(?).*

336. John wrote his third epistle. *Ephesus(?).*

337. Domitian became emperor of Rome. *Rome; 81 A.D.*

Note: **Persecution of the Christians During the Reign of Domitian**—In 81 A.D., at age 29, Domitianus, Vespasian's younger son, succeeded his brother Titus as emperor of Rome. He was a man filled with fear and suspicion; he terrorized Rome for fifteen years, using informers to ferret out suspected opponents in the army and senate. He began to press his claims as "master and god," and refusal to worship him was regarded as a sign of disloyalty. The Christians, who refused to regard him as a god, would not observe the required ritual acts such as burning incense before his statue. They insisted that they alone possessed the truth, and all other religions were false—including the state religions. Domitian persecuted the Christians with intensity. His reign ended abruptly on September 16, 96 A.D. when he was assassinated by a member of his own household.

338. John went to Rome, where an attempt was made to execute him by boiling him in a cauldron of oil, but he escaped unharmed. *Rome(?).*

Note: **Tertullian's Mention of John's Miraculous Deliverance**—This incident in John's life is alluded to by Tertullian, who wrote that John "was plunged, unhurt, into boiling oil, and then exiled on an island" (*Presc. Her.* 36).

339. John was banished to the Isle of Patmos. *Rome to Patmos(?); 95 A.D.*

Note: **Patmos**—The Romans used many isolated places to banish their exiles. Patmos is a tiny wind-swept island, only 25 square miles in area. It is in the Aegean Sea, off the coast of Asia Minor, about 28 miles south of Samos. Tradition holds that Domitian banished the Apostle John to the island in 95 A.D., and that he spent about 18 months there.

340. John wrote the book of Revelation (Rev. 1:9), and addressed it to seven churches in Asia Minor. *Patmos; 95-96 A.D.*

341. Domitian was assassinated, and Nerva became emperor of Rome. *Rome; 96 A.D.*

Note: **Nerva**—After Domitian's death, the Roman senate refused to give him a state burial, and they ordered his name removed from all public places because of his tyrannical rule. Then, for the first time in the history of Rome, the senate designated its own choice of an individual as the next emperor. The man the senate chose was a respectable old lawyer named Nerva. Knowing that his reign would be a short one because of his age, Nerva adopted a qualified candidate and trained him to be the next emperor. The result of his efforts was that Rome enjoyed a long period of tranquility. Nerva began the era of the "five good emperors." His successors were Trajan, Hadrian, Antoninus Pius and Marcus Aurelius. They followed the plan Nerva established for an orderly succession of the Roman emperors, and the Roman Empire reached its zenith during the reign of these men.

342. John was released, and returned to Ephesus. *Patmos to Ephesus(?); 96 A.D.(?).*

343. John died or was translated. *Ephesus; after 98 A.D.*

Note: **The Passing of John**—According to the history prepared by Eusebius, John remained in Ephesus and governed the churches in that area until after Trajan became the emperor of Rome. Polycrates (a bishop of Ephesus near the end of the second century), wrote in a letter to Hugo (bishop of Rome), that John was one of the "great lights" in Asia, and that "John, who was both a witness and a teacher, who reclined upon the bosom of the Lord, and, being a priest, wore the sacerdotal plate." He asserted that John had fallen asleep in Ephesus. There is no record of John's death; some scholars believe that he was translated, based on John 21:21-23.

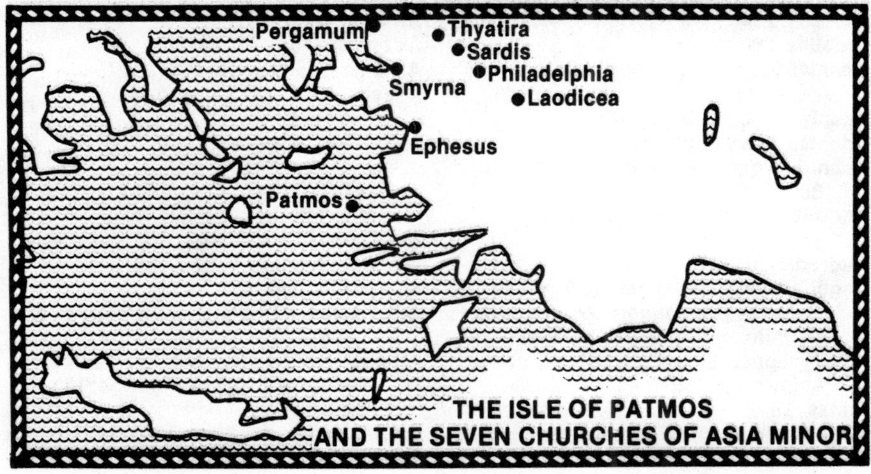

THE ISLE OF PATMOS
AND THE SEVEN CHURCHES OF ASIA MINOR

INDEX

EXPLANATION OF INDEXING SYSTEM

References in this index are listed in two ways. The majority of the entries consist of a number only (for example: 236) and refer to one of the 343 events in the history of the New Testament Church, which follow in chronological order throughout the book. Some references refer to the special helps included on various pages, and are listed by their page numbers preceded by a "p" for page (for example: p. 15).

A

K

L

M

Q

R

S